Decent Work, Green Jobs and the Sustainable Economy

Solutions for Climate Change and Sustainable Development

Decent Work, Green Jobs and the Sustainable Economy

Solutions for Climate Change and Sustainable Development

Peter Poschen

Published by Greenleaf Publishing Limited
Aizlewood's Mill
Nursery Street
Sheffield S3 8GG
UK
www.greenleaf-publishing.com

ISBN-13: 978-1-78353-518-7 [hardback]
ISBN-13: 978-1-78353-449-4 [paperback]
ISBN-13: 978-1-78353-447-0 [PDF ebook]
ISBN-13: 978-1-78353-448-7 [ePub ebook]

in association with
International Labour Office
4, route des Morillons
CH-1211 Geneva 22
Switzerland
www.ilo.org

ISBN-13: 978-92-2-129638-6 [print]
ISBN-13: 978-92-2-129639-3 [PDF ebook]
ISBN-13: 978-92-2-129640-9 [ePub]

Cover by Sadie Gornall-Jones

Printed and bound by Printondemand-worldwide.com, UK

British Library Cataloguing in Publication Data:
A catalogue record for this book is available from the British Library.

Contents

Figures

Tables

Boxes

Foreword

Over the coming decades, humanity will confront a series of severe environmental and social challenges which interact in a variety of ways. They range from pollution and the deterioration of many natural resources to climate change, from persistent high unemployment, working poverty and rising inequality to the lack of even basic social protection for most working people in the world.

Climate change has begun to take a serious and rising toll on economies, well-being and human lives. Over the last decade, erratic weather patterns and extreme weather events have decimated infrastructure, disrupted business activity, destroyed jobs and livelihoods, and killed people around the world on an unprecedented scale. Climate change has become the main driver of forced migration.

The world of work has cause to worry.

The challenges of achieving environmental sustainability and of generating adequate and decent work for all are closely linked. They therefore need to be addressed jointly, rather than understood as separate issues, let alone as incompatible goals. The greening of economies presents many opportunities to achieve social objectives: it has the potential to be a new engine of growth, both in advanced and developing economies, and a net generator of decent green jobs that can contribute significantly to poverty eradication and social inclusion.

As this book documents with reference both to specific experiences and to macroeconomic studies, positive outcomes are eminently possible. Their attainment requires a clear understanding of both opportunities and challenges, as well as country-specific policies that integrate environmental, social and decent work elements to ensure a smooth and just transition process.

The greening of enterprises and jobs and the promotion of green jobs can foster a productive, low-carbon, environmentally sustainable economy and contribute to the fight against climate change. It can enhance the resilience of vulnerable countries and communities. Managed well, the transition to environmentally and socially sustainable economies can become a strong driver of job creation, job upgrading, social justice and poverty eradication.

The International Labour Organization (ILO) and its constituents around the world have raised their voice. The message—amply reflected and illustrated in this book—is loud and clear: sustainable development is only possible with the active engagement of the world of work. The actors in the world of work—governments, employers and workers—are not passive bystanders, but rather agents of change, who are able to develop new ways of working that safeguard the environment for present and future generations, eradicate poverty and promote social justice by fostering sustainable enterprises and creating decent work for all.

Their voices and their engagement are needed more than ever at this crucial juncture. Governments must agree the Sustainable Development Goals (SDGs), the first truly global development agenda. Governments must conclude a new global agreement on climate change. And it is also clear that environmentally sustainable economies will be achievable only if people are given a clear stake in them and if the important contributions of millions of employers and workers around the world are enabled and duly valued in the agreements and in their implementation.

The world of work needs to weigh in on policy-making and on greening and climate resilience in enterprises and workplaces. This task will only grow over the decades to come as the SDGs and the new climate agreement need to be implemented.

ILO core competencies on employment, skills, enterprise development, labour markets, social protection, labour rights and social dialogue all play key roles in successfully tackling climate change and achieving sustainable development.

In order to fully support our constituents in the world of work in this enormous endeavour, I have launched an ambitious and long-term green initiative to fully integrate the environmental dimension into everything the ILO does, from research and policy advice to social dialogue and capacity building.

The ILO's role in the transition to a low-carbon, sustainable development path will be the single factor that will most clearly distinguish the Organization's second century of activity from its first.

Guy Ryder
ILO Director-General

Acknowledgements

This book could not have been written without the help of a large number of colleagues. Michael Renner and Steven Tobin were co-authors of the report *Working towards sustainable development* published by the Green Jobs Initiative in 2012, which laid the conceptual foundations and much of the analytical groundwork for the book. Michael Renner, Daniel Samaan, Valentina Stoevska, Kees van der Ree, Marek Harsdorff and Kamal Gueye provided significant inputs for the report on *Sustainable development, decent work and green jobs* prepared for the International Labour Conference in 2013, on which this book builds. Mito Tsukamoto, Helmut Schwarzer and Olga Strietska reviewed the text and made valuable suggestions for improvements. Thanks are due to Raymond Torres, Werner Sengenberger and José Manuel Salazar-Xirinachs for their encouragement and constructive feedback. Dorit Kemter and Anna Maria Fyfe made sure graphs, figures and references were correct. Gillian Somerscales carried out the final edit with great attention to detail. Last but not least, Charlotte Beauchamp ably coordinated the production of the book. I am deeply grateful to these colleagues for their support, but even more for their commitment and contributions to turn inclusive sustainable economies into a reality.

Abbreviations

AfDB	African Development Bank
BAU	business as usual
CHP	combined heat and power
CIC	Climate Innovation Centre
CO_2	carbon dioxide
EC	European Commission
EEA	European Environment Agency
EPWP	Extended Public Works Programme (South Africa)
EU	European Union
FAO	Food and Agriculture Organization
FTE	full-time equivalent
GDP	gross domestic product
GHG	greenhouse gas
GW	gigawatt
ICLS	International Conference of Labour Statisticians
ICT	information and communication technology
IEA	International Energy Agency
IILS	International Institute for Labour Studies
ILC	International Labour Conference
ILO	International Labour Organization/Office
IOE	International Organisation of Employers
IPCC	Intergovernmental Panel on Climate Change
IRENA	International Renewable Energy Agency
ITUC	International Trade Union Confederation
LDC	least developed country

LPG	liquefied petroleum gas
MDG	Millennium Development Goal
MGNREGA	Mahatma Gandhi National Rural Employment Guarantee Act (India)
NAPA	National Adaptation Programme of Action
NGO	non-governmental organization
OECD	Organisation for Economic Co-operation and Development
OSH	occupational safety and health
PAGE	Partnership for Action on Green Economy
PSNP	Productive Safety Net Programme (Ethiopia)
REDD	Reduced Emissions from Deforestation and Forest Degradation
SDG	Sustainable Development Goal
SHS	solar home systems
SME	small or medium-sized enterprise
STEM	science, technology, engineering and mathematics (skills)
UN	United Nations
UNCSD	UN Conference on Sustainable Development
UN-DESA	UN Department of Economic and Social Affairs
UNDP	UN Development Programme
UNEP	UN Environment Programme
UNFCCC	UN Framework Convention on Climate Change
UNIDO	UN Industrial Development Organization
UNITAR	UN Institute for Training and Research
USBLS	United States Bureau of Labor Statistics
WHO	World Health Organization

Executive summary

Making the economy environmentally sustainable is no longer optional, it is a necessity, in particular from the point of view of labour markets and social development. Economic activities are increasingly exceeding planetary boundaries; extreme weather events and overuse of natural resources are already leading to losses of jobs and incomes. ILO estimates put the economic loss from climate change at over 7 per cent of world output by 2050. Organisation for Economic Co-operation and Development (OECD) and World Bank projections are even higher. There is a real danger that many of the past gains in development and poverty reduction could be undone.

Given the scale and urgency of these environmental and employment challenges, it is clear that the world will have neither the resources nor the time to tackle them separately or consecutively. Tackling them jointly is not an option, but a necessity. An integrated approach that treats the environment and social development as closely interrelated pillars of sustainable development turns the drive towards environmental sustainability into a significant avenue for development.

A growing body of experience and research from countries at all levels of development shows that **a well-managed transition to environmentally and socially sustainable economies offers three major opportunities:**

1. It could generate a **net gain of up to 60 million additional, good quality jobs** compared with a "business as usual" (BAU) development path.

2. It could **significantly improve the quality of jobs and lift hundreds of millions out of poverty.**

3. Access to affordable clean energy, energy-efficient housing and transport can become a vehicle for social inclusion for over 1 billion people.

It is, however, essential also to recognize and address three challenges for **the world of work** that arise from a transition to a greener economy. First, the restructuring entailed by **a shift to low-carbon, resource-efficient economies can lead to job losses**, particularly in energy- and resource-intensive sectors. While research suggests that these changes are much smaller than those caused by globalization and technological change over the last decades, they are likely to affect sectors, communities and workers that have already felt the impacts of earlier restructuring and often have few economic alternatives. Second, **climate change is already disrupting, and will increasingly disrupt, economic activity**, destroy assets and undermine jobs and livelihoods; adaptation is essential for communities, enterprises and workers. Third, many of the policies formulated to achieve environmental sustainability, such as **carbon pricing or energy subsidy reform, tend to be socially regressive**; these effects can and should be compensated for.

It is important to recognize the interactions between economic sectors and the fact that no single measure, economic sector or country can achieve environmental sustainability. Therefore, opposing "green" and "non-green" is not useful. **Greening concerns all enterprises, economic sectors and countries.**

The **greening of economies** presents many opportunities to achieve social objectives: it **has the potential to be a new engine of growth**, in both advanced and developing economies, and **a net generator of decent green jobs** that can contribute significantly to poverty eradication and social inclusion. **To realize this potential, the transition needs to be just and well managed.**

This book presents a wealth of analysis and experiences at national, sector and enterprise level which show how just transitions can be achieved. **The concepts, analytical tools, dialogue mechanisms, policy instruments, business strategies and workplace practices to bring about a successful and just transition exist.** It is increasingly recognized that **workers in green jobs are indispensable for achieving environmental sustainability** in all economic sectors and most enterprises.

Policies matter. Positive outcomes require coherent sets of country-specific policies articulating economic, environmental, sectoral and enterprise policies with social and labour market policies, in particular social protection, skills and active labour market policies. Policies need to be mindful of the gender dimensions of both the opportunities and the challenges of the transition. If policies are gender sensitive, the transition could go a long way to empower women economically and to alleviate their burdens.

Environmental tax reform stands out as a policy instrument for generating a double dividend for the environment and labour markets. **Suitable analytical tools are available** to understand the interactions and carry out the necessary country-specific analysis and policy design, including input–output models, social accounting matrices and dynamic models.

Governments can support enterprises and create an enabling environment which promotes the adoption of green workplace practices, investments in new green products and services, and the creation of jobs. A number of cases documented in this book demonstrate that **impressive results have been achieved by enterprise efforts and workplace cooperation between management and workers to reduce environmental impacts.**

Governments, employers and workers are agents of change, not passive bystanders. The numerous and diverse national, sectoral and enterprise initiatives presented in this book demonstrate that they are all able to develop new ways of working that safeguard the environment for present and future generations, eradicate poverty and promote social justice by fostering sustainable enterprises and creating decent work for all. The world of work has a growing range of solutions to offer for sustainable development and dealing with climate change.

A growing number of countries at all levels of development, as well as economic sectors and individual enterprises, are embarking on transitions to environmental sustainability, a green economy or green growth. For these countries and enterprises, the conclusions of the 102nd Session of the International Labour Conference (ILC) in 2013 set out a vision and guiding principles for a just transition. They also organize the relevant policy areas into a coherent policy framework for achieving just transitions.

Unanimously adopted by the government, employer and worker representatives of 185 ILO member States, **the ILC's 2013 conclusions give specific, internationally agreed meaning and guidance for the implementation of the SDGs and the global climate agreement** to be reached in 2015. The agreement of operational definitions to capture the greening of the economy and green jobs adopted by the International Conference of Labour Statisticians (ICLS) in 2013 and initiatives for data-gathering will soon help in setting targets and monitoring progress.

Sustainable development as envisaged by the Rio+20 summit, including the shift to a low-carbon economy, and the implementation of the SDGs and of a global climate agreement are only possible with the active engagement of the world of work.

Introduction

Two defining challenges for the twenty-first century

This book addresses two of the defining challenges of the twenty-first century: ensuring environmental sustainability; and turning the vision of decent work for all into a reality as a basis for dignified and fulfilled lives for individuals, with social cohesion and stability for communities and countries.

Environmental degradation and resource depletion have become ever more visible and pressing challenges, as the human population keeps expanding and material demands increase, pushing against the limits of what the planet can provide sustainably. The overuse of natural resources, such as forests, fish and clean water, is increasingly exceeding planetary boundaries. The biggest environmental challenge by far, and one that threatens to undermine the very basis of human civilization if allowed to continue unchecked, is climate change. The climate crisis also connects in powerful ways with many other environmental concerns such as water availability or biodiversity.

At the same time as environmental concerns have risen to unprecedented prominence, there are also urgent social and economic challenges. Even as the size of the world economic product has more than tripled since 1990, securing adequate and decent employment for all jobseekers remains one of the biggest problems policy-makers face, especially in the wake of the global financial crisis, which expanded the ranks of the unemployed and those in vulnerable employment conditions. The number of unemployed people rose from 170 million, before the onset of the world financial crisis in 2007, to a projected 206 million in 2014, and may further rise to 215 million by 2018. Youth unemployment was pegged at 74.5 million in 2013 and is not expected to fall significantly over the next five years.[1]

It should be noted that the unemployment rate has significant shortcomings in indicating the true degree of workforce underutilization, in the form of disguised and unrecorded unemployment and of underemployment. Furthermore, the same rate of unemployment can create highly different degrees of social damage, depending on a country's social protection systems (Sengenberger, 2011).

Over the past two decades, there has been a vigorous debate over the precise nature of the relationship between the environment and the economy. As climate action grows urgent, some observers warn that economies will suffer as a result of moving towards sustainability. But it has become clear that economic prosperity and employment depend in fundamental ways on a stable climate and healthy ecosystems. This book shows that both the environmental and the socio-economic challenges are urgent and that they are intimately linked. They can and must be addressed together.

Not only is the situation environmentally unsustainable, it has substantial economic and social costs. The natural processes and systems which are vital to the enterprise and the livelihoods of people are being disrupted, and the damage to economies and to society caused by environmental degradation and climate change threatens to undo many of the gains in development and poverty reduction achieved over the past decades, including progress towards achieving the Millennium Development Goals (MDGs). The longer we wait to address this, the worse it will get: with global unemployment levels exceeding 200 million, almost one in three workers living in working poverty and 5.1 billion people without access to essential social security, the addition of rising costs and disruption associated with environmental damage could further weaken social cohesion and increase the instability already present in a number of countries.

Employment that contributes to protecting the environment and reducing humanity's heavy environmental footprint offers people a tangible stake in a green economy. The pursuit of so-called green jobs will be a key economic driver as the world steps into the still relatively uncharted territory of building a low-carbon global economy. "Climate-proofing" the economy will involve large-scale investments in new technologies, equipment,

1   ILO (2014) and supporting data sets at http://www.ilo.org/global/research/global-reports/global-employment-trends/2014/WCMS_234879/lang--en/index.htm.

buildings and infrastructure, which will provide a major stimulus for much-needed new employment and an opportunity for protecting and transforming existing jobs.

Environmental constraints, climate change and the transition to a sustainable, low-carbon economy will have profound impacts on production and consumption patterns, and on enterprises and workers. The necessary shift will be impossible without a pervasive effort towards the greening of enterprises across the economy. In addition, reducing greenhouse gas (GHG) emissions implies shifts within and between economic sectors as well as between regions. Output and employment in low-carbon industries and services, in waste management and recycling, and in the restoration of natural capital will grow. Energy and resource-intensive sectors, on the other hand, are likely to stagnate or even contract. With well-designed adaptation measures, climate resilience can go hand in hand with job creation and poverty reduction. Green jobs can serve as a bridge between current MDG 1 (eradicate extreme poverty and hunger) and MDG 7 (ensure environmental sustainability) and future SDGs 1 (end poverty in all its forms everywhere) and 8 (promote sustained, inclusive and sustainable economic growth, full and productive employment and decent work for all).

The ILO and its constituents—governments, employers and workers—have a history of active engagement and support for sustainable development. The multiple economic, social and environmental crises besetting the world in recent years have led to a new sense of urgency. The United Nations (UN) Conference on Sustainable Development (UNCSD) held in Rio de Janeiro in 2012 (Rio+20) discussed the green economy in the context of poverty reduction, sustainable development and environmental governance. The outcome document of this largest UN conference ever stresses the urgency of sustainable development and the fundamental role of decent work in achieving it. This is the culmination of a remarkable evolution in the way the relationships between the environment, the world of work and social development are considered in policy statements, both at the UN and at the ILO.

Recognizing the pivotal role of decent work for sustainable development

While the UN Conference on Environment and Development, or Earth Summit, in Rio de Janeiro in 1992 emphasized the need for balance between the economic, social and environmental dimensions of sustainable development, the outcome document contained very limited coverage of labour issues and was largely silent on their relationship to sustainable development. The UN Framework Convention on Climate Change (UNFCCC), one of the three environmental conventions adopted in Rio, made no reference at all to employment and labour issues. The otherwise comprehensive Agenda 21 also produced by the summit merely called for countries to "generate remunerative employment and productive occupational opportunities compatible with country-specific factor endowments, on a scale sufficient to take care of prospective increases in the labour force and to cover backlogs" (UN, 1993, para. 3.8(a)). Agenda 21 did, however, recognize the importance of the social partners among the major stakeholder groups: Chapters 29 (workers) and 30 (employers) set out their respective roles in dealing with sustainable development issues at the national and workplace levels. It should be noted, though, that this scant coverage of labour issues is largely a reflection of the lack of available analysis and data at the time concerning the relationship between employment and skills development and sustainable development.

Ten years later, the World Summit on Sustainable Development in Johannesburg (2002) still inserted only a short paragraph into its declaration and the Johannesburg Plan of Implementation.

It was only after the World Summit on Social Development in 2005 adopted full employment and decent work as a global goal, and the subsequent inclusion of a set of employment indicators under MDG 1, that the role of decent work in sustainable development started to receive consistent recognition.

At the ILO too, the close interlinkages between the environment and the world of work came to be increasingly acknowledged (ILO, 2007a), and the general discussion and conclusions on sustainable enterprises reinforced the insight that "it is in workplaces that the social, economic and environmental dimensions of sustainable development come together inseparably" and also called for just transitions for workers affected by economic restructuring (ILO, 2007b, paras 3 and 8).

A 2007 report by the Director-General of the ILO discussed the relationship between decent work and the environment, and referred for the first time to the concept of green jobs. The Green Jobs Initiative—a partnership between the UN Environment Programme (UNEP), the International Trade Union Confederation (ITUC), the International Organisation of Employers (IOE) and the ILO—was launched in 2007. Its mission was to promote opportunity, equity and a just transition to sustainable economies, and to mobilize governments, employers and workers to engage in dialogue on coherent policies and effective programmes leading to a green economy with green jobs and decent work for all. In 2008, the initiative published its first report, a ground-breaking analysis of the relationship between decent work and the environment (UNEP, ILO, IOE and ITUC, 2008).

The following year, the Global Jobs Pact was adopted by the ILO in response to the global financial and economic crisis, and called for cooperation on "shifting to a low-carbon, environment-friendly economy that helps accelerate the jobs recovery, reduce social gaps and support development goals and realize decent work in the process" (ILO, 2009a, para. 21(3)).

The social partners also integrated the interrelationships between employment and labour issues and the environment into their own policies and programmes. The IOE adopted a policy on climate change in 2008 and has been active in providing services to members as well as participating in the Green Economy Task Force with the International Chamber of Commerce, which published the first Green Economy Roadmap produced by business as a "comprehensive framework for policies and action for business, policy-makers, and society to accelerate and scale up a transition toward a 'green economy'" (ICC, 2012). More than 2,300 companies have signed up to the ICC's Business Charter for Sustainable Development.[2] The ITUC adopted a landmark resolution on combating climate change through sustainable development and just transition at its Second Congress in 2010 (ITUC, 2010).

In 2010, the parties to the UNFCCC included a specific reference to decent work in the "shared vision" for a future global climate agreement. In the Cancún Agreements (UNFCCC, 2010), governments recognized that "addressing climate change requires a paradigm shift towards building a low-carbon society that offers substantial opportunities and ensures continued high growth and sustainable development ... while ensuring a

2   See International Institute for Sustainable Development website at http:// www.iisd.org/business/tools/principles_icc.aspx.

just transition of the workforce that creates decent work and quality jobs". Similar language has been proposed by parties for the text of a new global climate agreement to be reached at the end of 2015.

Rio+20 in 2012 was attended by more than 100 Heads of State and Government and over 400 ministers. The Rio+20 outcome document sets out a vision of sustainable development with social inclusion. It firmly establishes the pivotal role of decent work for sustainable development, both in a dedicated chapter and through numerous cross-references, emphasizing that it is vital to understand and act on the interlinkages between the economic, social and environmental pillars. It identifies the concept of a green economy as one of the pathways to sustainable development and stresses that its goal must be social inclusion and the creation of employment and decent work for all:

> we consider green economy in the context of sustainable development and poverty eradication as one of the important tools available for achieving sustainable development and that it could provide options for policymaking but should not be a rigid set of rules. … We emphasize that it should contribute to eradicating poverty as well as sustained economic growth, enhancing social inclusion, improving human welfare and creating opportunities for employment and decent work for all, while maintaining the healthy functioning of the Earth's ecosystems. (UNCSD, 2012, para. 56)

While this international consensus has been emerging, a rapidly growing number of governments and enterprises have been acting on the need to achieve synergies and manage trade-offs between growth, employment and social inclusion and the preservation of the environment.

Recognizing the economic and social aspects of environmental change

New thinking is also permeating international organizations, including those with a mandate centred on economic development. In recent years, the World Bank (World Bank, 2012a), the International Monetary Fund (IMF, 2011), the OECD (OECD, 2010), the UN Industrial Development Organization (UNIDO) (UNIDO, 2009), the G20 (G20, 2012) and the World Economic Forum (WEF, 2012) have all published reports and adopted strategies calling for new ways of defining and achieving development that are built around environmental sustainability and greener economies as a central tenet. They conclude that investing in the environment to increase its productivity, protect its stock of resources and harness its services is indispensable, makes economic sense and underpins growth. These organizations therefore regard green economic growth, or a green economy, as superior to conventional growth in the medium to long term.

In February 2012, the UN Statistical Commission approved the System of Environmental and Economic Accounts. This new internationally agreed standard fits alongside the current System of National Accounts, which is restricted to measuring gross domestic product (GDP). It mainstreams natural capital into economic accounts, and governments in several countries, including Australia, Mexico and the Philippines, are already using it to evaluate trade-offs between different policies and to assess their impacts across the economy, the environment and society. In the same way that private businesses look at assets and liabilities on their balance sheets, countries are enabled to account for their assets and natural stocks.

New opportunities for promoting decent work for all

The emphasis on sustainable development with decent work as a central goal in an environmentally more sustainable economy provides a major opportunity for the ILO to advance its mission. However, while analysis of the relationship between the economic and the social dimensions of sustainable development has been a mainstay of the Organization since its foundation and extensive policy guidance is available in this regard, an understanding of the policy implications of pursuing both environmental sustainability and decent work is less well developed.

This book therefore focuses on the links between the environmental and the social dimensions of sustainable development, including their economic implications. It summarizes the growing body of evidence that the shift to a more environmentally sustainable economy is not only indispensable,[3] including from a labour market perspective, but can in fact lead to net gains in employment, significant improvements in job quality and incomes, and advances in equity and social inclusion on a large scale.

These benefits are not automatic, but contingent on the right policies. Similarly, appropriate and coherent policies can mitigate the challenges

3   This report draws heavily on ILO and IILS (2012a), which presents the evidence in greater detail, in particular concerning key economic sectors.

environmental sustainability poses for the world of work. The ILO constituents can leverage the process of structural change towards more sustainable patterns of production and consumption into a global transition to decent work for all. At the same time, observing ILO policies and international labour standards can attenuate environmental degradation and serve to meet the goals of environmental sustainability. For example, if compliance with basic worker rights prevents forced labour, child labour or the suppression of free trade unions, lower tolerance of environmentally hazardous production and materials can be expected.

This emphasis should, for example, be reflected in the international development agenda emerging for post-2015. The central role assigned to decent work in the Rio+20 outcome document should ensure that decent work will be considered in the formulation of sustainable development goals initiated in Rio.

Clear understandings of the interrelationship between environmental sustainability and decent work, of good policy practices and of effective institutional mechanisms will also be crucial for effective national policy and a major contribution to the international efforts to achieve sustainable development.

The structure and content of this book

Chapter 1 analyses the environmental and social challenges facing the world against the backdrop of the current economic crisis. It explores the relationship between them and introduces concepts which help to evaluate social and labour market impacts. Chapter 2 identifies three major opportunities to advance decent work in a greener economy in the form of more jobs, better jobs and social inclusion. Chapter 3 explores three challenges linked to a transition to a greener economy from a world of work perspective, notably restructuring, employment losses and relocation of workers; the pressing need to adapt to climate change; and inadvertent negative impacts on income distribution. Chapter 4 outlines relevant policy initiatives at national and international levels, gives an overview of current ILO work in this area, and summarizes policy lessons from national experiences and research. Chapter 5 provides a summary of major findings and lessons learned.

1
Sustainable development and decent work

The transition towards a more environmentally sustainable and socially inclusive economy entails reorienting growth to ensure that equal weight is given to the economic, social and environmental dimensions when setting objectives. In this respect, the ILO's Decent Work Agenda has the potential to serve as a coherent policy framework, to the mutual benefit and improved integration of macroeconomic, investment, employment, social protection and environmental policies and objectives. However, to achieve such a framework, it will be necessary to translate the concept of sustainable development into practical policy and ensure that the three dimensions of this concept are simultaneously and equally addressed.

Indeed, the environmental challenges and the social challenges are inextricably linked. Economic growth, job creation and incomes depend on—and can degrade—natural resources and systems. However, they can also restore and enhance environmental sustainability. Given the scale and the urgency of the challenges, it is clear that the world will have neither the resources nor the time to tackle them separately or consecutively. They need to be addressed together, in a comprehensive and complementary manner. The questions are, then, whether and how an environmentally sustainable economy can offer opportunities to create decent work and improve social inclusion.

1.1 Environmental challenges: their economic and social cost

Since the first UN Conference on the Environment in 1972, the world's population has almost doubled to over 7 billion. Meanwhile, the world economy has more than tripled in size. While this growth has pulled hundreds of millions out of extreme poverty, the benefits have been unevenly distributed and achieved at significant cost to the environment. Future economic growth with decent work, rising living standards and improved human well-being will critically hinge on preserving, managing and restoring the natural assets on which all life and economic activity depend. Failure to do so will have serious consequences, especially for the poor, and will ultimately undermine the economic growth and human development prospects of future generations (ILO and OECD, 2012).

The BAU scenario of "grow first and clean up later" is not sustainable. Escalating natural resource use and pollution will compound the growing scarcity of fresh water and fertile land and accelerate the loss of biodiversity and climate change beyond tolerable levels. If not addressed quickly and decisively, these environmental challenges will increasingly undercut economic growth and jobs. This cost is obvious in the case of immediate impacts such as large-scale pollution from environmental disasters, but is even higher for the less perceptible, insidious, "slow onset" phenomena such as biodiversity loss and climate change, which cause damage that is often irreversible.

It is important to bear in mind that these challenges are often interrelated, and can give rise to positive feedback loops that exacerbate undesirable outcomes. Indeed, the OECD in its *Environmental outlook to 2050* argues that "there is compelling scientific evidence that natural systems have tipping points or biophysical boundaries beyond which rapid and damaging change becomes irreversible" (OECD, 2012a, p. 26). It warns that further delay in addressing environmental challenges risks very costly—even, in certain cases, catastrophic—changes. Estimates available for some of these economic and social costs highlight that they are indeed significant.

1.1.1 Natural resource use

The International Resource Panel has analysed the economic effects of scarcity of natural resources (UNEP, 2010a). In a 2011 report it examined the extraction of four categories of primary raw materials—construction minerals, ores and industrial minerals, fossil fuels and biomass (UNEP, 2011a). It found that, in total, these materials are mined and harvested at a rate of 47–59 billion tonnes per year. A BAU scenario would lead to a tripling of global annual resource extraction by 2050.[1]

A recent study by the McKinsey Global Institute has shown that intensive resource use drives up energy and commodity prices (Dobbs et al., 2011). It argues that a complete rethinking of resource management, with sharp increases in energy and material efficiency, will be needed to reconcile limited resources with soaring demand. In particular, demand increases of 30–80 per cent across all major resources will coincide with increasing difficulty and cost of finding and extracting them. The study points out that the sharp increase in commodity prices between 2000 and 2011 has wiped out the price declines of the previous 100 years. Moreover, it suggests that the global economy could face several decades of higher and more volatile resource prices, which could have adverse consequences on output. The slump in prices for energy and some commodities since 2009 in the wake of the "great recession", along with subdued economic growth coupled with cheap finance and massive investment in shale gas extraction, could be seen as an instance of this volatility. Already, the overuse of resources has led to the sharp contraction or collapse of some industries in G20 countries, such as forestry in China, Indonesia and the western United States, or fishing in parts of Canada, with associated job losses ranging from tens of thousands to almost 1 million.

1.1.2 Pollution

In the absence of increased efficiency, reuse and recycling, global waste volumes will continue to escalate rapidly, adding to the pollution of soil, water and air. The World Bank estimates that global annual production of waste will reach 2.2 billion tonnes by 2025, nearly double the most recent figure of 1.3 billion tonnes (World Bank, 2012b).

Pollution of air, water and soil is a persistent problem for the health of humans and ecosystems at both local and global levels. According to the OECD, exposure to hazardous chemicals is already significant on a worldwide scale and is likely to increase in the coming decades, particularly in emerging economies and developing countries. The concentrations of pollutants in some cities already exceed safe levels (OECD, 2012a).

1   This BAU scenario assumes no major system innovation such as faster efficiency improvement or a switch away from fossil energy.

Unabated increases in pollution are likely to lead to a doubling of premature deaths caused by airborne particulate matter in urban areas, to 3.6 million per year by 2050, most of them occurring in China and India. At the same time, the benefit:cost ratio of acting on pollution can be as high as 10:1 in emerging economies (OECD, 2012a). Respiratory problems resulting from pollution could also increase, particularly in urban areas. Meanwhile, indoor air pollution from burning biomass, coal and kerosene is responsible for 4.3 million premature deaths each year, according to new figures from the World Health Organization (WHO) that are substantially higher than previous estimates (WHO, 2014). Most of the victims are women and children (WHO, 2011). Pollution trends in general are likely to widen existing inequalities and deepen vulnerability among the poor. Pollution also may diminish the working capacity of the labour force and coerce workers into premature retirement, thereby adding to expenditure on social security.

1.1.3 Water scarcity and land degradation

Fresh water is already scarce in many parts of the world. Water stress is projected to increase, with water supplies predicted to satisfy only 60 per cent of world demand in 20 years' time (Water Resources Group, 2009). The OECD's *Environmental outlook to 2050* projects that, by 2050, 2.3 billion more people will be living in areas experiencing severe water stress, bringing the total to over 40 per cent of the world's population. Water shortages will hinder the growth of many economic activities. Industry, power generation, human consumption and agriculture will increasingly compete for water, with serious implications for food security.

Irrigation for food production in agriculture already takes about 70 per cent of available water. And, while agricultural yields have increased thanks to the use of chemical fertilizers, more intensive farming reduces soil quality and contaminates water resources. Water and food shortages also tend to increase the workload of women (UNDP, 2010a).

1.1.4 Biodiversity

The wealth of plant and animal species provides the basis for food production and raw materials for a host of commodities and products, from textiles and building materials to paper and pharmaceuticals. The number and the diversity of species are critical for the stability of ecosystems. Today, species become extinct at a rate between 100 and 1,000 times higher than what could be considered natural (Rockström et al., 2009). Up to 30 per cent of all mammal, bird and amphibian species will be threatened with extinction this century (Díaz et al., 2005). While the main drivers of biodiversity loss have been land-use change and management (agriculture, commercial forestry, urbanization) and pollution, climate change is projected to become the fastest-growing driver of biodiversity loss by 2050 (OECD, 2012a).

In spite of their vital functions and the enormous scale of their value, ecosystem services[2] and biodiversity are often overlooked: their value and the cost of their loss are not systematically reflected in national accounts and are rarely transmitted as market signals into business decision-making. Initial findings from The Economics of Ecosystems and Biodiversity (TEEB) series put the annual cost of losses in biodiversity and ecosystem services due to deforestation and forest degradation at the equivalent of US$25 trillion (EC, 2008). This is equivalent to over 30 per cent of world GDP in 2011.

Several hundred million people depend on forest, marine and coastal biodiversity for their livelihoods. The World Bank estimates that, in 43 low-income countries, natural capital makes up 36 per cent of total wealth, even without factoring in the wider range of services that ecosystems provide (World Bank, 2012c).

The availability and sustainable use of biodiversity by the poor are directly relevant to poverty eradication. For example, in Brazil, India and Indonesia, the standard contributions to GDP of agriculture, forestry and fisheries combined, reflecting only the traded goods in the markets, were 6.1 per cent, 16.5 per cent and 11.4 per cent respectively in 2005. For the rural poor, the share is much higher: 89.9 per cent, 46.6 per cent and 74.6 per cent respectively (EC, 2008).

For developing countries, the cost of these forms of environmental degradation, taken together, is very significant and offsets much of the economic growth achieved. World Bank studies of 21 developing countries found the annual cost to range from 2.1 per cent of GDP in Tunisia to 9.6 per cent in Ghana, with a weighted average of 8 per cent (Fay, 2012; see also Croitoru and Sarraf, 2010).

2   "Ecosystem services" are the benefits that people obtain from ecosystems. These include supporting services such as nutrient recycling, primary biomass production and soil formation which are fundamental for the production of all other ecosystem services; provisioning services such as food and water; and regulating services such as regulation of floods, drought, land degradation and disease.

1.1.5 Climate change

One of the most serious global threats, and one which aggravates other environmental concerns such as water scarcity and biodiversity loss, is climate change. In the medium to long term, climate change leads to an increase of average global temperatures, changes in rainfall regimes and an increase in sea levels. In the short term, climate change impacts include the results of erratic weather patterns and more extreme weather events. Climate change is primarily caused by increased concentrations of GHGs[3] in the atmosphere, arising mainly from the burning of fossil fuels and biomass, animal husbandry, rice-field irrigation and use of nitrogenous fertilizers. These GHGs trap more of the energy reaching the earth from the sun, for roughly 59 per cent of total emissions. Industrial activity (i.e. manufacturing) and transport are also two major sources, accounting for 21 and 14 per cent respectively.

Emissions from fossil fuel burning, cement production and land-use changes are up 42 per cent over 1990 levels, and they increased 2.7-fold, to 10.75 billion tonnes of carbon, between 1960 and 2013 (Le Quéré et al., 2014). Global average temperatures are today 0.8°C higher than before the onset of the industrial revolution, with a 0.7°C rise since 1951. As a result, the melting of glaciers in the Arctic and on Greenland has led to a global average sea-level rise of 10–20 centimetres in the past 100 years,[4] while weather patterns have become more erratic and extreme weather events more devastating.

Per capita GHG emissions are still highest in high-income countries, at on average about ten times those of developing countries in 2011, although in 2013 China, with 7.2 tonnes of carbon per capita, surpassed the European Union (EU), with 6.8 tonnes (UNEP, 2011b; Nicola, 2014).

Under BAU scenarios, continuously rising emissions could drive concentrations of GHGs in the atmosphere from the present-day level of 390.5 ppm CO_2 (Blasing, 2014) to 685 ppm by 2050, with probable consequent warming of 3–6°C. This concentration and attendant range of temperature

3   Mostly carbon dioxide (CO_2), nitrous oxide (NO_x), methane (CH_4) and a group of fluorinated gases.

4   Comparison of the rate of sea-level rise over the last 100 years (1.0–2.0 mm/yr) with the geological rate over the last two millennia (0.1–0.2 mm/yr) implies a comparatively recent acceleration in the rate of sea-level rise.

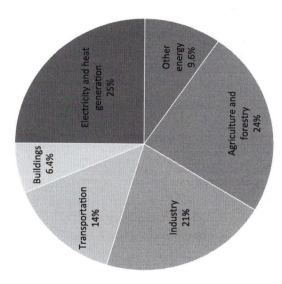

FIGURE 1.1   Shares of global greenhouse gas emissions, by sector (percentages)

Source: IPCC (2014).

increases, far exceeding the internationally agreed maxima of 450 ppm and 2°C (OECD, 2012a), would have serious and possibly unmanageable consequences. Because GHGs remain active in the atmosphere for long periods of time, global temperatures and sea levels will continue to rise for centuries even after GHG concentrations have been stabilized. The challenge for the future is therefore to radically and quickly reduce emissions as well as to adapt to the climate change which is already occurring and will continue for decades due to GHG emissions already released.

Modelling undertaken by the International Institute for Labour Studies (IILS) supports the conclusion that much higher concentrations of GHGs in the atmosphere will entail considerable costs in terms of output and aggregate productivity levels. In particular, the IILS Global Economic Linkages model, which simulates behaviour by enterprises, suggests that productivity levels in 2030 would be 2.4 per cent lower than in 2010 and 7.2 per cent lower by 2050 in a BAU case (see figure 1.2). The negative effect is related to the impact of extreme weather conditions on agriculture and infrastructure, to scarcity of fresh water resources and to issues related to human health. Besides directly lowering output, this distortion also lowers the productivity of capital and labour. If the model were adjusted to include the cost to individual well-being, the cost of inaction would rise further. Unmitigated

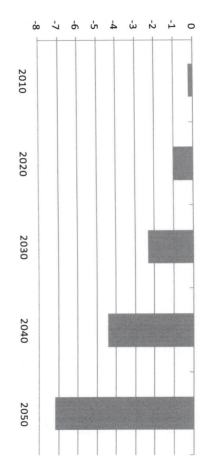

FIGURE 1.2   Productivity loss resulting from further increases in greenhouse gas compared to the baseline, 2010–50 (percentage points)

Note: The baseline scenario assumes that environmental damages remain at the level of the base year (2000).

Source: Bridji, Charpe and Kühn (2011).

climate change could lead to a permanent loss of global consumption per capita of 14 per cent by 2050 (OECD, 2012a). Living standards would be significantly affected as a result.

These estimates are in line with a number of studies assessing the economic damage resulting from climate change. Lord Stern, the former chief economist of the World Bank, estimated the permanent loss of global economic output at 0–3 per cent for warming of 2–3°C and 5–10 per cent for 5–6°C (the current BAU scenario) (Stern, 2007). Global consumption would be reduced by between 5 and 20 per cent over the next 200 years. According to Nordhaus, economic damage from climate change would increase to 3 per cent of global output by 2100 and close to 8 per cent by 2200 on current emission trends (Nordhaus, 2007). Average annual damage from 2000 to 2200 would amount to US$26 trillion (Ackerman and Stanton, 2006).

In addition to the economic costs of policy inaction, there will be other effects on social well-being, such as rising health costs. For example, findings from the UNFCCC show that global warming—through its impact on disease vectors—could expose an additional 400 million people to the risk of malaria before the end of the twenty-first century (UNFCCC, 2007).

Already, there is growing evidence of the dramatic effects that severe weather that may be linked to global warming can have on economies and societies. As climate change continues to alter weather patterns, unpredictable weather conditions remain the most significant factor causing volatility in the price of agricultural products (OECD and FAO, 2011). High prices for maize and soybean (FAO and WFP, 2012) following drought in the United States in 2012 illustrate the nature and the scale of the problem. The number of people suffering from malnutrition and hunger stands at 805 million worldwide, of whom 791 million are in developing countries (FAO, 2013). The food price increases in 2008 pushed more than 105 million people into poverty (World Bank, 2012d) and triggered food riots in a number of countries.

There are also direct losses of jobs and incomes. For example, as a result of Hurricane Katrina in the United States in 2005, New Orleans lost some 40,000 jobs; the hardest hit were women, mostly African American (OECD, 2008). Cyclone Sidr in 2007 disrupted several hundred thousand small businesses and adversely affected 567,000 jobs in Bangladesh; the estimated value of non-agricultural private assets fell by some US$25 million (ILO, 2008). In both cases, poorer households were more exposed because they live in more vulnerable areas and have fewer resources to enhance resilience to climate change. Climate change is likely to have a particularly marked effect in magnifying existing patterns of gender disadvantage (UNDP, 2007). Worldwide, women have less access than men to financial, institutional and other resources that would enhance their capacity to adapt to climate change, including access to land, credit, agricultural inputs, decision-making bodies, technology and training services (Aguilar, 2008). In many countries, droughts, floods and deforestation increase the burden of unpaid work on girls and women, leaving them less time for education or earning an income. The situation is even worse for women attempting to recover from environmental disasters.

1.2 Social challenges and economic instability: their link to the environment

The risks to livelihoods from the environmental challenges outlined above compound the many existing social challenges, including unemployment. According to the UN Development Programme (UNDP), about 1.75 billion people experience multidimensional poverty in health, economic opportunities, education and living standards (UNDP, 2010b).

With an additional 36 million people joining the ranks of the unemployed since 2007, in 2014 the worldwide total of unemployed stood at 206 million.

With unemployment at this record level, 400 million young people will be entering the global labour market over the next decade in search of employment opportunities. Currently, 75 million people aged 16–25 are unable to find a job, and young people account for more than a third of total unemployment (ILO, 2014).[5] To generate sustainable growth while maintaining social cohesion, the world must therefore rise to the urgent challenge of creating 600 million productive jobs over the next decade (ILO, 2012a).

In addition to massive unemployment, poor job quality and working poverty pose even larger challenges. Some 900 million workers—almost 30 per cent of all workers—are living with their families below the US$2 a day poverty line, most of them in developing countries and in precarious and informal employment.

A significant proportion of these workers are employed in sectors which are threatened by the overuse of natural resources and climate change, such as agriculture, forestry and fisheries, which together have a global workforce of well over 1 billion. Most of the 1.4 billion people still living on less than US$1.25 a day (UN-DESA, 2009) depend for their jobs and livelihoods on these sectors. The continued marginalization of employment and incomes in these sectors will further accelerate migration out of rural areas and increase pressure on urban labour markets. Many urban poor live in precarious settlements and work in informal businesses exposed to storms, floods and landslides. ILO analysis has shown that poverty is increasingly feminized, with about 829 million girls, young adult and older women living below the poverty line compared with about 522 million males (ILO, 2009b). Overuse of natural resources and accelerated climate change would lead to massive increases in deprivation in both rural and urban enterprises and labour markets.

These risks are aggravated by the lack of social protection, which could help vulnerable sectors and groups to absorb economic and environmental shocks such as harvest failures, soaring food prices, increased exposure to disease or loss of assets from floods and storms. About 5.1 billion people, 75 per cent of the world population, are not covered by adequate social security which would provide basic income security and access to health care (ILO, 2011a, b). A basic level of social security, guaranteeing at least basic income security and access to essential health care through national social

5   Supporting data sets available at http://www.ilo.org/global/research/global-reports/global-employment-trends/2014/WCMS_234879/lang--en/index. htm.

protection floors, would not only reduce the suffering but become a step-ping stone facilitating access to productive employment, breaking the circle of multidimensional poverty.

There is also a lack of access to economic opportunity and to fundamental services. A case in point is the lack of access to clean and affordable energy suffered by 1.3 billion people, mostly in sub-Saharan Africa and South Asia, which also acts as an important impediment to social inclusion and pro-ductive work, in particular for women.

The jobs and social protection deficits go hand in hand with a prolonged investment deficit in both public and private sectors. World investment as a share of GDP fell to a record low in 2009, and at 24.5 per cent in 2013 is still below pre-crisis levels (IMF, 2014). Most of the persisting investment short-fall originates in the advanced economies—notably the EU, where contin-ued efforts to redress budget deficits are having a negative impact on public investment and the overall business climate.

At the same time, global stock indices have far surpassed the levels achieved in 2007, providing ample resources to large firms. Small firms, by contrast, continue to have difficulty accessing credit—in the advanced economies owing to the credit crunch, in many developing economies owing to a lack of formalization and suitable financing mechanisms.

Both environmental and social drivers can lead to large-scale, non-linear and disruptive environmental and social change, from the collapse of farming systems to the "Arab Spring" uprisings triggered by the lack of opportunity for youth. But the interlinkages between economic and social factors can also lead to positive synergies, as will be seen in many examples throughout this book. A clear and stable policy framework for sustainable development which addresses the environmental challenges could signifi-cantly contribute to addressing the economic and social woes. Targets and strategies for energy and resource efficiency in agriculture, industry, trans-port and housing, the generation of clean, universally accessible energy, and the restoration of natural resources would significantly stimulate demand and prompt private investment on a massive scale.

In such a context, social protection systems would not be exposed to the risk of runaway costs from environmental degradation and an ever-increasing share of expenditure to compensate for and limit damages, but would serve as a powerful vehicle for social and economic inclusion as well as environmental sustainability.

While increased pressure on farmers and a growing gap between the incomes of rural and urban populations could worsen the employment and poverty challenges, investments in rural infrastructure such as water management and social protection can create jobs and restore soil and water catchment areas, thus enhancing resilience to climate change, improving agricultural productivity and boosting incomes.

1.3 The drive to environmental sustainability and its implications for decent work

The imperative of addressing environmental challenges has been increasingly recognized by governments, the private sector and citizens at large. Initially, the measures adopted were often aimed at remedying acute environmental problems with obvious and immediate local impacts on human health, such as water and air pollution. The selected examples below and the detailed overview in Chapter 4, as well as in Annex I, Table A2, demonstrate that, over the last decade, more and more governments and businesses around the world have been tackling these and other environmental challenges.

1.3.1 An environmentally sustainable economy: the shift to sustainable patterns of production and consumption

Governments have been adopting national strategies for climate change, preservation of biodiversity, land and water management, waste management and recycling, and shifting to sustainable production and consumption patterns. Businesses are responding by making their operations, products, services and supply chains more sustainable.

The furthest-reaching approach has inverted the traditional logic that preserving the environment is a cost and an impediment to economic growth. Green economy strategies, or "green growth" as they are called by some countries and organizations, see environmental sustainability as a major economic opportunity, a driver of investment, economic growth and job creation. These concepts have been developed and promoted by leading international agencies in the fields of economics and the environment, including UNEP, the World Bank and the OECD (see box 1.1).

The green economy concept championed by UNEP is explicit about the goal of human well-being and social equity, with environmental investments as drivers of income generation and employment creation. While the World Bank refers to the need for social inclusion, it is less explicit about the mechanisms through which green growth would achieve this. The OECD,

Box 1.1: Definitions of green economy and green growth

UNEP: "UNEP defines a green economy as one that results in 'improved human well-being and social equity, while significantly reducing environmental risks and ecological scarcities'. In its simplest expression, a green economy is low-carbon, resource efficient, and socially inclusive. In a green economy, growth in income and employment are driven by public and private investments that reduce carbon emissions and pollution, enhance energy and resource efficiency, and prevent the loss of biodiversity and ecosystem services."

The World Bank: "We argue that what is needed is green growth — that is, growth that is efficient in its use of natural resources, clean in that it minimizes pollution and environmental impacts, and resilient in that it accounts for natural hazards and the role of environmental management and natural capital in preventing physical disasters. And this growth needs to be inclusive."

OECD: "Green growth means fostering economic growth and development while ensuring that natural assets continue to provide the resources and environmental services on which our well-being relies. To do this it must catalyse investment and innovation which will underpin sustained growth and give rise to new economic opportunities."

Sources: UNEP (2011c), p. 16; World Bank (2012a), p. 2; OECD (2011), p. 9.

for its part, had originally put forward green growth as a way of continuing economic growth while preserving vital natural resources. The outcome document of UNCSD 2012 considers the

> green economy in the context of sustainable development and poverty eradication as one of the important tools available for achieving sustainable development and that it could provide options for policy-making but should not be a rigid set of rules. We emphasize that it should contribute to eradicating poverty as well as sustained economic growth, enhancing social inclusion, improving human welfare and creating opportunities for employment and decent work for all, while maintaining the healthy functioning of the Earth's ecosystems.
> (UNCSD, 2012, para. 56)

Both concepts have gained currency in a growing number of countries in recent years. The Republic of Korea has made green growth the central theme—and the title—of its national development strategy. Expanding on the "Green New Deal", a package of measures to counteract the economic crisis, the government has embarked on a longer-term "Green Growth Strategy". Some 91 trillion won (about US$84 billion) have been invested between 2009 and 2012, and the number of green jobs was projected to rise from 610,000 in 2008 to 810,000 in 2013 (Republic of Korea, 2012). However, the policy also has its critics, who argue that large companies will benefit much more than small or medium-sized enterprises (SMEs); that there is a high proportion of short-term irregular positions among the green jobs created; and that a main pillar of the package, the "Four Major Rivers Restoration" project, is more of a construction project than a green project (Kim, Han and Park, 2012).

Ethiopia and South Africa have adopted green economy strategies as components of their development plans. Because the conventional development path would lead to an unsustainable use of natural resources as well as a sharp increase in GHG emissions, Ethiopia aims to achieve middle-income status by 2025 while developing a green economy (Government of Ethiopia, 2011, 2013). The government's "Climate Resilient Green Economy" strategy rests on four pillars (crops and livestock; forests; renewable energy; and energy-efficient technologies). Most of the investment of around US$200 billion required over the next 20 years is cost-effective, directly driving economic growth and creating additional jobs with high value added. South Africa has included green economy investments as one of ten components in a comprehensive "New Growth Path", a strategy that aims to create 5 million additional jobs by 2020 (Borel-Saladin and Turok, 2013). In November 2011, representatives of government, private business, labour unions and civil society joined to sign the "Green Economy Accord", with the hope of creating at least 300,000 green jobs. A number of other countries have also recently adopted green growth strategies, including Cambodia, Chile and Vietnam.

The Employment Package of the EU (EC, 2012) relies on growth in environmental industries as one of three components (the others being health and care, and information and communication technology (ICT)). Green jobs are the second largest source of new employment in the package, accounting for up to 8.2 million jobs across the EU. In July 2014, the European Commission (EC) followed up with a Green Employment Initiative that laid out an integrated framework for employment policies in the transition to a green economy. The initiative is focused on six priority areas: bridging skills gaps; anticipating and securing transitions; supporting job creation; increasing data quality and monitoring; promoting social dialogue; and strengthening international cooperation (EC, 2014).

The Confederation of British Industry summarizes developments in the United Kingdom: "In trying economic times, the UK's green business has continued to grow in real terms, carving out a £122 billion share of a global market worth £3.3 trillion [in 2010/11] and employing close to a million people" (CBI, 2012, p. 6). In the United States, the production of green goods and services employed 3.1 million workers (2.4 per cent of the workforce) in 2010. In particular, the "clean tech" segment expanded rapidly and outperformed the rest of the economy during the recession (Muro et al., 2011).

China has increasingly embedded environmental sustainability in national development policy since 1984 and counts over 4 million green jobs today. The new five-year economic development plan (adopted in May 2012) sets out strategic targets and measures for green, low-carbon and circular[6] economies. The plan identifies priority industries, including alternative forms of energy, energy conservation and environmental protection, biotechnology, high-end equipment manufacturing and clean-energy vehicles. China expects these industries to account for 15 per cent of the country's GDP by 2020, up from 2 per cent a decade earlier. This is expected to create new green jobs as part of a net gain of 10 million jobs (CCICED, 2011).

Brazil and Indonesia have adopted unilateral targets to reduce GHG emissions and are implementing programmes across a range of sectors, from agriculture and forestry to energy and transport. The Indonesian Government is committed to maintaining economic growth, creating jobs in particular for youth and reducing poverty while improving environmental sustainability and reducing carbon emissions levels. An integrated development strategy with four prongs—pro-growth, pro-jobs, pro-poor and pro-environment—is being implemented under the national medium-term development plan (RPJMN) for 2010–14, integrating the environmental dimension in all aspects of policy-making. Increasingly, the drive towards environmental sustainability and the related opportunities to create green jobs are reflected in employment policies. In Sri Lanka, for example, the National Human Resource and Employment Policy adopted in October 2012 aims at full, productive and freely chosen employment for all, and explicitly identifies key sectors for employment and environment.

1.3.1.1   Policy instruments for environmental sustainability

By combining policy instruments, governments can provide incentives for the adoption of green workplace practices and for investment in new green products and services. The policy tools adopted are an important determinant of the nature and the extent of the impact that measures for environmental sustainability will have. Such tools can include:

6   A circular economy applies a "cradle to cradle" flow: materials are not discarded after use but reused, recycled and/or transformed into new products.

- **Market-based instruments** such as taxes, charges, tradable permits, guaranteed prices, subsidies and loans on favourable terms. These instruments reinforce market signals such as rising prices for scarce commodities or growing consumer demand for green products and services. They can stimulate technological innovation and competitiveness, providing incentives for private investment and for the greening of enterprises. Existing subsidies on water, energy and raw materials which impede environmental efficiency in enterprises and households can also be modified or reduced. Ensuring success requires, however, an efficient system of monitoring, revenue collection and enforcement.

- **Regulatory instruments** such as norms, standards, emissions abatement policies, quotas and mandates, as well as national/regional laws and regulations. These ensure, for example, that biomass and other renewable materials are produced sustainably.

- **Public investment**: in many instances this leads the development of infrastructure with low environmental impact or the rehabilitation of natural resources such as forests, rivers or coastal areas.

- **Public procurement policies**: when purchasing goods, for example, governments can favour those product designs that are more environmentally sound.

- **Information-based instruments** such as eco-labelling, awareness raising and public disclosure. These can also be efficient if used with other measures such as environmental taxes. The establishment of supporting institutions for industries, assisting enterprises in meeting standards and obtaining certifications, can be helpful.

- **Voluntary initiatives**: these can lower administrative and enforcement costs (when compared with regulatory instruments, for instance).

1.3.2 A more environmentally sustainable economy: repercussions for the world of work

The move towards a more environmentally sustainable economy has implications for the volume and quality of employment and for the level and distribution of incomes, particularly when it involves a wholesale shift of the economic development models of large companies, sectors and entire countries. It is likely to lead to employment gains and losses and to the transformation of many jobs throughout the economy.

1.3.2.1 Enterprises and workplaces

Both resource scarcity and climate change can drive up costs and threaten the viability of an enterprise. This is particularly true if technology, production processes and practices are inefficient. Wasted resources mean low resource productivity, and this reduces profits and competitiveness. Over the past decades, productivity improvements in the use of raw materials and energy have been much slower than those in labour productivity in industrialized countries (see figure 1.3). Labour productivity has also outpaced materials and energy productivity in some emerging economies, but here the gains have been very substantial, doubling or tripling over the last three decades.

Numerous studies, including two extensive reviews by the McKinsey Global Institute, have shown that major gains in efficiency are possible and that many of these are already cost-effective with today's technology

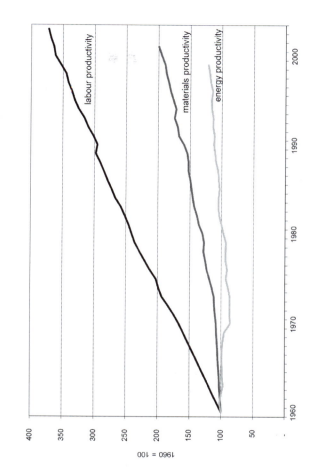

FIGURE 1.3   Labour, materials and energy productivity, EU-15, 1960–2000
Note: Labour productivity: GDP per annual working hours (1999 US$ (converted at EKS PPPs) per hour); materials productivity: GDP per domestic material consumption (DMC) (€ per kg); energy productivity: GDP per total primary energy supply (TPES) (thousand 1995 US$ per tonne).

Source: EEA (2005).

and prices. Realizing these gains requires investment in new technology, but also adjustment in processes and practices. As Rosenfeld et al. point out, meeting the energy challenge will not be possible without the active involvement of millions of managers, workers and consumers (Rosenfeld et al., 2009; Dobbs et al., 2011).

Individual firms as well as governments are driving environmental sustainability at the enterprise level. The highly successful programme "Pollution Prevention Pays" at the multinational 3M, for example, has saved the company US$1.4 billion since 1975. In China, the government has recently launched a "Top 10,000" initiative which promotes awareness and skills for energy savings and emissions reductions at the 16,078 enterprises with the highest environmental footprint (NDRC, 2012).

Both reaping the gains of energy and resource efficiency and avoiding pollution and major industrial accidents depend critically not only on technology but also on management systems, operational procedures, good communication, and skilled and motivated workers. As The Economist magazine put it in relation to nuclear power plants: "safety can never be a technological given, only an operational achievement" (The Economist, 2012).

Where good environmental performance is achieved it becomes a comparative advantage. In addition to reducing cost and providing technological leadership, it increases brand value and can give better access to capital and to consumer markets.

1.3.2.2 Key economic sectors employing half the global workforce
There is no "silver bullet" for achieving environmental sustainability. Given the scale and the multiple facets of the challenge, no single measure, group of enterprises or sector can reduce the environmental footprint of economic activity enough to ensure overall sustainability. Greening will be required to varying degrees in all enterprises across the entire economy.

The sectoral composition of a national economy is an important determinant of both the challenges and also the potential for economic development and environmental sustainability, and for the likely impact on enterprises and workers. Those economic sectors that are directly dependent on natural resources and the climate, or are large consumers of resources or significant polluters or a combination of these, have significant potential to reduce environmental impact. Eight sectors stand out because of their close relationship to environmental sustainability: agriculture, forestry, fisheries, energy, resource-intensive manufacturing, recycling, buildings and transport. As will be seen in the following chapters, many of the environmental policies adopted to date, and also the more comprehensive green economy or green growth strategies, focus on these sectors.

Enterprises in a given sector share a number of relevant features which influence the transition to sustainable production and consumption patterns in the sector and its social outcomes: the types of product and service they provide, the technological options and constraints imposed by the activity, the occupational hazards and working conditions associated with the nature of the activity, the levels of productivity, and the sets of relevant technical and vocational skills. There are also broad similarities in employment and workforce patterns and composition, such as seasonal work, gender composition and the structure of the sector in terms of sizes of enterprises.

Sectors also have specific governance instruments and institutions. A significant number of international labour standards and national labour laws are specific to individual economic sectors. Because of these shared features, employers and workers are usually organized and engage in dialogue and collective bargaining at the sectoral level.

Both governments and the private sector typically concentrate their efforts on a limited number of these key sectors because of their current relevance for the national economy or because of their potential to boost national development. The policy instruments and measures adopted are often sector-specific. From a world of work perspective it is important to note that, together, these sectors employ half the global workforce. A very large proportion of the workforce will therefore be directly affected by the drive to achieve sustainability (see table 1.1).

Sector	Direct employment
Agriculture	1,000
Forestry	44
Fisheries	25
Energy	30
Manufacturing (resource-intensive)	200
Recycling	24
Buildings	110
Transport	88
Total	1,521
Percentage of global employment	50.08

TABLE 1.1   Global direct employment, by sector (millions)

Source: UNEP, ILO, IOE and ITUC (2008).

Some of these sectors are experiencing growth and increases in employment because their products and services contribute to environmental sustainability. In contrast, some sectors with a large environmental footprint are faced with slower growth or even contraction. In order to understand and monitor the impact of a transition to a greener economy for employment it is therefore helpful to distinguish between green industries (subsectors such as renewable energy, or parts of sectors such as energy-efficient construction) and non-green industries.

In green industries, all the employment in the sector contributes to environmental sustainability. However, industries such as shipbreaking or recycling may be characterized by environmental hazards, sweatshop practices and non-decent working conditions. Shipbreaking is typically outsourced to low-cost countries in order to avoid more stringent environmental and labour standards elsewhere. Generally, such standards help determine whether, and to what degree, a particular industry can be considered to be providing green and decent jobs.

In non-green sectors, there are nevertheless some workers in green occupations, responsible for monitoring and limiting negative environmental impacts. Examples are operators of wastewater treatment plants in pulp mills, or logistics and facilities managers reducing energy consumption of transport fleets and buildings. Both the employees of green industries and those in green occupations directly reduce environmental impacts. These are therefore considered green jobs. The concept and its relevance for the contribution of the world of work to environmentally sustainable development are set out in greater detail in Section 1.4.1 and explored throughout this book.

1.3.2.3 National economics

In addition to the enterprise and sectoral levels of analysis, a third level which is relevant for this discussion is the national economy as a whole, including its links to the global economy. Enterprises do not exist in isolation but are part of value added chains from which they source their inputs and into which they sell their products and services. This is true for green industries as well, which require many inputs from non-green industries. Price signals, whether as a result of resource scarcity or of policies penalizing pollution or encouraging environmentally friendly products, affect the behaviour of consumers and enterprises throughout the economy. This creates a complex interplay which determines labour market balances in terms of net gains or losses in employment and the volume of job reallocation associated with the transition. It may also have an impact on job quality and the level and distribution of income.

It is important to note that this is a two-way relationship. As the *World Development Report 2013* points out: "Development happens through jobs" (World Bank, 2012e, p. 8). This also applies to the environmental dimension of sustainable development. Investment in human and social capital, the creation of green jobs and the greening of enterprises are key elements of a growth and sustainable development agenda because they drive and enable environmentally sustainable development.

1.4 The labour market dynamics of greening economies: green jobs creation, employment and income effects

The shift to an environmentally sustainable economy has given rise to green jobs, a new type of job which plays a vital role in greening enterprises and economies. The definition and measurement of green jobs are instrumental in understanding the interrelationship between environmental sustainability and labour markets.

1.4.1 Creating green jobs

The joint UNEP/ILO/IOE/ITUC report of 2008 broadly defined a green job as any decent job that contributes to preserving or restoring the quality of the environment, be it in agriculture, industry, services or administration (UNEP, ILO, IOE and ITUC, 2008). In practice these jobs:

- Reduce consumption of energy and raw materials
- Limit GHG emissions
- Minimize waste and pollution
- Protect and restore ecosystems
- Enable enterprises and communities to adapt to climate change

The dividing lines between green and non-green are not always easily discernible, and sector- and technology-specific assessments may be required for a determination. Energy and materials efficiency is a central, yet dynamic factor. Technologies and products considered efficient at one point in time may not be considered efficient at a later stage, as more effi-cient alternatives emerge. Often, the full environmental impact of new tech-nologies, materials and products is revealed only after considerable time, and perhaps even only at the end of the lifetime of a product, including the way waste is disposed or treated.

An important element in this definition of green jobs is the fact that the jobs have to be not only green but also decent, i.e. jobs that are produc-tive, provide adequate incomes and social protection, respect the rights of workers and give workers a say in decisions which will affect their lives. This definition incorporates the three dimensions of sustainable development. Green jobs are those entailing decent work which significantly reduces negative environmental impacts of economic activity, ultimately leading to sustainable enterprises and economies (see box 1.2).

Box 1.2: Decent work and environmental sustainability: definitions, issues and considerations

A better understanding of the impacts of a greener economy on labour markets and enterprises, and an assessment of the effectiveness of policy measures and business strategies, require consistent data collection and measurement. These need to be based on a clear conceptual framework and an operational definition. Such definitions have been developed and applied in a growing number of countries.

In response to the need for conceptual and practical guidelines for the measurement of green jobs, guidelines for a statistical definition of employment in the environmental sector and green jobs were presented and adopted by the 19th International Conference of Labour Statisticians (ICLS) in 2013. These guidelines set out a basis for collecting comparable data and producing internationally harmonized statistics.

According to the ICLS guidelines, employment in the environmental sector includes persons involved in the production of environmental goods and services as well as workers whose duties involve making their economic units' production processes more environmentally friendly or make more efficient use of natural resources.

A distinction is made between employment in production of environmental outputs and employment in environmental processes, defined respectively as follows:

1. **Employment in production of environmental outputs** is defined as employment in the production of environmental goods and services for consumption outside the producing unit. It may exist in specialist or in non-specialist economic units. Employment in production of environmental outputs in non-specialist economic

units, or specialist units that have non-environmental secondary activities, cannot be measured directly unless the jobs are linked with the types of product produced. Linkage of this type would be costly and difficult to implement in data collection. In the absence of such information this type of employment can be approximated, using, for example, the data on the value of environmental goods and services produced as a proportion of the value of the total production. For non-market producers (e.g. government units), the proportion of their employment contributing to the production of environmental goods and services can be estimated by using other relevant variables such as the share of wages and salaries or of working time spent on production of environmental output.

2. **Employment in environmental processes** is defined as employment in the production of environmental goods and services for consumption within the producing unit. It may exist in specialist economic units and in economic units that are not environmental in nature (i.e. non-specialist or own-account producers). These are jobs in which workers' duties include production of environmental goods and services for use within the economic unit, but also the use of methods, procedures, practices or technologies that make their economic units' production processes more environmentally sustainable.[7] Where possible a distinction should be made between those workers who spend less than 50 per cent and those who spend more than 50 per cent of their working time on environmental processes.

The term "green jobs" refers to a subset of employment in the environmental sector that meets the requirements of decent work (i.e. adequate wages, safe conditions, workers' rights, social dialogue and social protection).

These three concepts complement each other and shed light on different ways of greening enterprises and economies, offering different entry points for policies. Figure 1.4 presents these relationships schematically, specifically:

A. Employment in production of environmental outputs

B. Employment in environmental processes

C. Decent jobs

D. Jobs in non-environmental sectors created thanks to greening

---

7   This includes methods, procedures, practices, or technologies that, for example reduce or eliminate pollution, reduce consumption of water and energy, minimize waste, or protect and restore ecosystems. This type of employment also includes jobs in which workers are employed to research, develop, maintain or use technologies and practices to reduce the environmental impact of their economic unit, or to train the unit's workers or contractors in these technologies and practices.

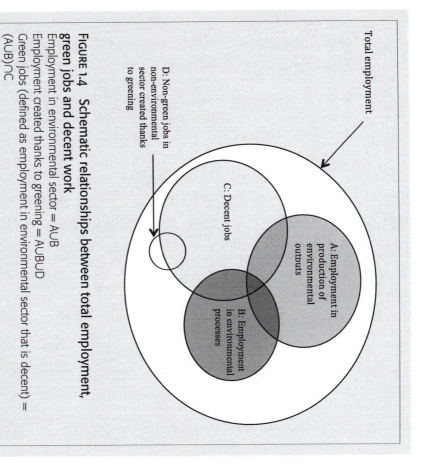

Total employment

D: Non-green jobs in non-environmental sector created thanks to greening

C: Decent jobs

A: Employment in production of environmental outputs

B: Employment in environmental processes

FIGURE 1.4   Schematic relationships between total employment, green jobs and decent work

Employment in environmental sector = AUB
Employment created thanks to greening = AUBUD
Green jobs (defined as employment in environmental sector that is decent) = (AUB)∩C

Related concepts include the following:

- Employment in the non-environmental sector created thanks to greening; this refers to employment in economic units that supply goods and services to the environmental sector. Such employment may be estimated using input-output tables and environmental expenditure data.

- Employment in low-carbon economic units and energy-efficient enterprises: this refers to employment in units that have low carbon emissions (e.g. employment in green buildings) and to employment in enterprises that are more energy efficient than most of the enterprises within the same economic activity.

- "Green work", this refers to all work involved in production of environmental goods and services. It includes employment, voluntary work and own-use production work[8] to produce environmental goods and services.

---

8   Refers to production where the output is intended mainly for consumption or use by the person producing it, or by members of that person's household or family members living in other households.

Most practical applications have taken an industry approach, identifying green jobs with employment in industries that are judged to produce green products and services

Source: ILO, 2013a; ILO, 2013b.

On the one hand, green jobs are an important part of the employment gains linked to a more environmentally sustainable economy. On the other hand, they are critical for making the shift technically feasible and economically viable. Without skilled and motivated workers in new green growth sectors and in key occupations across the economy, the investment made and the technology deployed will not generate the expected benefits for sustainable development.

1.4.1.1 Employment dynamics and balances

On a positive note, increased demand for and investment in greener products and services, as well as the equipment and infrastructure to produce them, will lead to the expansion of certain industries and enterprises. This will translate into higher labour demand and job creation (direct jobs), primarily in green sectors. In addition, due to inter-industry relations among the expanding industries, other parts of the economy which supply inputs to the expanding green sectors also benefit, creating additional employment (indirect jobs), including in non-green sectors such as high-insulation glass and cement for green buildings, or steel and carbon fibre for the blades and towers of wind turbines. The income generated by this additional economic activity is redistributed by spending on additional consumption and investment across the economy, creating further employment (induced effects) in addition to the direct and indirect jobs.

The number of jobs created at all stages of the greening process in a national economy is a function of the scale of demand and investment, of trade (where products themselves or inputs are imported, subtracting from domestic demand, or exported, thereby increasing domestic demand and related employment), of intersectoral dynamics, and of employment elasticity (jobs created or maintained per unit of demand). Using the example of France, figure 1.5 illustrates that this shift can be very favourable in terms of job creation. Demand for green goods and services tends to have higher employment elasticities than average demand and is substantially greater than demand for resource- and energy-intensive goods (with the exception of car maintenance).

FIGURE 1.5   Direct and indirect employment (full-time job equivalents) generated per € million final demand for goods and services from selected sectors, France, 2005

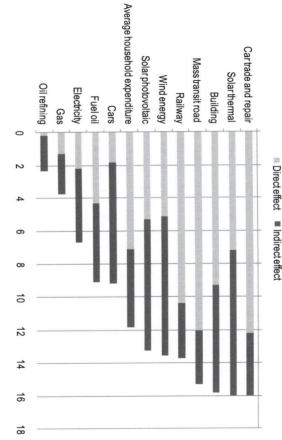

Source: Quirion and Demailly (2008).

A further conditioning factor is "budget effects". If green products and services are more expensive than their substitutes, enterprises and households will have fewer resources left to spend on other goods and services. A negative budget effect can, for example, be associated with the introduction of renewable energy. Although the cost of power generation using renewables has been falling fast and has become increasingly competitive, it initially resulted in higher costs to consumers, albeit temporarily.

Conversely, positive budget effects do occur, for example, due to cost-effective investments in energy efficiency and broader resource efficiency (Rosenfeld et al., 2009; Dobbs et al., 2011). The resulting gains shift demand away from energy consumption, which has a low employment elasticity, to goods and services with higher elasticities. Importantly, these gains are cumulative over time. Thus, the potential for job creation is not limited to certain industries but can occur throughout the economy, with some significant spillover effects. Together, these add up to the gross gains in employment.

However, this mechanism also has a downside since, for every job lost, employment (and income) will be adversely affected in other parts of the economy, because a given green product or service replaces a less green

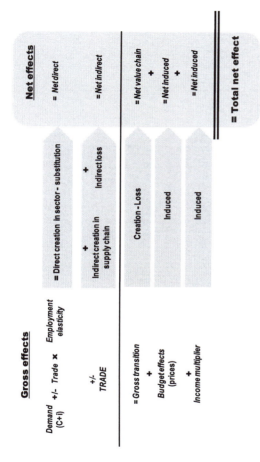

FIGURE 1.6 Impact of a green economy on the volume and composition of employment

Source: ILO and IILS (2012a).

one. An increase in renewable energy, for example, may reduce demand for conventional fossil power and thus for fossil power plants, as well as having an impact on supply sectors such as coalmining. The direct, indirect and reduced losses add up to a gross loss in employment.

Both the gross and the net effects are important. Taken together, the gross gains and losses are equivalent to the number of workers who will have to change jobs. This is an indication of the size of the transition occurring in the labour market. The direct and indirect gains and losses also help to explain the nature of the transition, as they show whether workers are likely to have to move between sectors or whether the relocations will take place mainly within the same sector. The net effects are equally important because they show whether or not a greener economy will generate more jobs or result in job losses (see figure 1.6). Whether the overall, quantitative effect on employment is positive or negative depends on the complex interplay between these job flows and the policy mix (see also Chapter 2).

1.4.1.2 Changes in employment quality, income levels and distribution

The transition will not only cause shifts in the overall level and composition of employment, but can also affect the quality of employment. Working conditions can change as a result of new technologies, processes and practices. These may reduce or increase exposure to occupational hazards, for example. The current focus on the transition to a low-carbon economy should look at complex environmental problems from a multidisciplinary approach, integrating environmental aspects with occupational safety and health (OSH) and public health, while at the same time taking into consideration the well-being of surrounding communities.

Environmentally sustainable products and services will often require higher levels of skills. Higher environmental performance and competence requirements in firms and sectors may also call for more stable and formal employment and enterprises. Green growth sectors and occupations may offer more or less equal opportunity to women and men or to certain groups of jobseekers. Similarly, these jobs may provide more or less opportunity to exercise the right to organize and bargain collectively.[9]

In addition to the impacts on employment, the shift to a green economy will also affect levels and distribution of income, with implications for poverty reduction. Gains in eco-efficiency and access to new and growing markets can lead to higher profits, incomes and wages. Conversely, additional costs which cannot be compensated may depress earnings. These impacts are a result of how the shifts in employment affect primary incomes, most importantly the levels of wages among workers and incomes among the self-employed, as well as the redistribution of incomes through taxation, social protection and prices.

Changes in taxation and prices can have strongly differentiated impacts on households of different income levels, as well as on women and men. An important case in point is energy poverty. While rich households consume more energy than poor households in absolute terms, in most countries the poor spend a disproportionate share of their income on energy and an even higher share on related goods and services, such as food and transport. For instance, in much of Africa, Asia, Latin America and parts of Europe, the proportion of expenditure on energy by poor households is three times—and can be as much as 20 times—that of richer households. The situation is aggravated by the fact that many poor households have no access to modern energy, energy-efficient housing or transport (ILO and IILS, 2012a). Meanwhile, the bulk of energy subsidies benefit richer households. In Mexico, the richest 20 per cent of households receive more than half of all gasoline subsidies, but the poorest 30 per cent of households only 0.9 per cent. For LPG (liquefied petroleum gas), the picture is only somewhat less

9   The evidence in the renewable energy sector, for instance, is decidedly mixed: see Renner, 2013; ITUC, DGB and Friedrich Ebert Stiftung 2014.

lopsided, with 32 per cent of subsidies going to the richest households, and 17 per cent to the poorest (Tovar, 2014).

The following chapters explore the opportunities and challenges for the world of work presented by a transition to more environmentally sustainable economies.

2 Seizing the opportunities: lessons from international experience

This chapter explores three distinct opportunities to promote decent work in the transition to greener, environmentally sustainable economies and societies: by creating more decent jobs, by improving the quality of existing jobs and by advancing social inclusion. It highlights the state of knowledge concerning countries and sectors which have already experienced the creation of more and better jobs and improved access to new opportunities for hitherto excluded segments of society. It sheds light on the size and scope of the opportunities in greener economies, and assesses the net effects for employment. Finally, it reviews a range of policies that are conducive to positive outcomes for the labour market and decent work.

2.1 Evidence of the positive employment effects of green policies

2.1.1 Job creation

Most studies at global, regional and country level that have investigated the net impact on employment of environmental policy measures suggest it is positive.[1] A review of 30 studies available for 15 countries and the EU

---

1 A number of studies which argue that environmental policies destroy jobs apply inappropriate methods and use data selectively.

(see Annex I, table A1), and one global analysis,[2] find that appreciable net employment gains have been or can be achieved. The results depend, not surprisingly, on the policy measures taken, the methodological approach adopted, country-specific circumstances and the data used in the analysis. In the majority of studies, environmental reforms are accompanied by complementary government policies and incentives, including tax credits, subsidies and worker training and education. By complementing environmental reform with labour market and social policies, any negative effects of environmental reforms are offset and the net impact on employment is positive. These findings are in line with the double-dividend hypothesis, according to which policy measures can achieve economic benefits—in particular, employment gains—and environmental improvement at the same time. According to the ILO/IILS study at the global level, for instance, modelling shows that up to 14 million net new jobs could be created if a tax on CO_2 emissions were imposed and the resulting revenues were used to cut labour taxes (ILO and IILS, 2009).

The OECD has simulated an illustrative emissions reduction scenario with a cross-country, multisector general equilibrium model (ENV-Linkages) to assess impacts on growth, employment and incomes in OECD countries (Chateau, Saint-Martin and Manfredi, 2011). In an economy where wages do not adjust fully to falling demand, growth and employment would fall by up to 2 per cent, unless the revenue from an emissions tax or an emissions trading scheme were recycled. By contrast, in a moderately "rigid" labour market, an environmental tax reform which recycles the revenue to reduce the cost of labour would increase OECD employment by 0.8 per cent above BAU levels by 2030, while maintaining real incomes. The sharpest increases would occur in renewable energy industries.

In emerging economies such as Brazil, China, Mauritius and South Africa, green investments were found to accelerate economic growth and employment creation. A 2010 study by the World Bank for Brazil, for example, found that by adopting a low-carbon development path, including avoiding emissions from land-use change (reducing pasture areas and protecting forests), energy efficiency and renewable energy, GDP would grow 0.5 per cent per year above the BAU scenario between 2010 and 2030, while employment creation would be 1.13 per cent faster over the same period (World Bank, 2010).

2   This section is a brief summary of the findings. For a more detailed presentation and discussion, see ILO and IILS (2012a), ch. 10.

The 30 studies span a range of advanced and emerging countries and use a variety of different analytical approaches. The scenarios analysed range from economy-wide emissions reductions to increased recycling and rehabilitation of natural resources. In spite of this diversity the findings converge, with most indicating net gains in employment of 0.5–2 per cent. This would translate into 15–60 million additional jobs, based on today's labour force.

Most analysis has taken relatively modest existing or envisaged environmental policies as the driver, and employment outcomes as a passive result. Studies on Australia, Germany, the EU as a region and the United States have investigated the effects of more ambitious environmental targets and suggest that substantially larger employment gains are possible. They could make a significant contribution to reducing unemployment.

In one of the studies, the Australian Conservation Foundation and the Australian Council of Trade Unions commissioned an economic modelling exercise to assess how best to protect jobs across all regions of Australia under the impact of climate change and climate-change policies (ACF and ACTU, 2009). The model assesses the effects of two different approaches— a "weak action" scenario and a "strong action" scenario. The weak action scenario is a "markets only" approach. It assumes a price on GHG pollution (using an emissions trading scheme) as the sole instrument to reduce Australia's pollution levels. The strong action scenario is a "markets plus" approach, where an emissions trading scheme is complemented by a targeted suite of policies to reduce GHG pollution domestically. The study reveals that both methods not only reduce CO_2 emissions but also increase employment compared to BAU, with 770,000 additional jobs under the strong action scenario. This would yield an employment gain of 5–6 per cent by 2030.

In the search for ways out of the recent financial and economic crisis, an interdisciplinary group of researchers analysed a more ambitious environmental policy for Germany. This would lead to a strong push in environmental investment, lifting GDP growth for 2010–20 to over 2 per cent instead of little over 1 per cent per year in the absence of new policies. This would create about 2 million additional jobs (a rise of 5 per cent of total employment) relative to BAU. Unemployment would fall by only 1 million because more people without a job would be encouraged to look for work again. A concerted approach with other EU countries would lead to significantly better outcomes than a "Germany alone" approach (Jaeger et al., 2009).

A 2011 study on the countries of the EU concludes that the employment outcomes from ambitious climate protection policies could be significantly more positive: "In the coming decade, Europe will need to accept the challenge of increasing economic growth while reducing both unemployment and greenhouse gas emissions" (Jaeger et al., 2011, p. 5). New model results show that these three goals can actually reinforce one another: "over the coming decade raising the EU's climate target from 20 per cent to 30 per cent can foster the following outcomes":

- Increase the growth rate of the European economy by up to 0.6 per cent per year

- Create up to 6 million additional jobs Europe-wide

- Boost European investments from 18 to 22 per cent of GDP in 2020

- Increase European GDP in 2020 by 5.7 per cent over BAU while reducing emissions by 11 per cent

In the green growth scenario, unemployment in the EU-27 would stand at 13.4 million by 2020 (5.3 per cent), as opposed to 19.4 million (7.6 per cent) under BAU—almost one-third lower (Jaeger et al., 2011, p. 80).

Another, more recent, study focusing on the EU assessed the employment and labour market impacts of the EU's Energy Roadmap to 2050, which aims to achieve 80–95 per cent reductions in GHG emissions. The study applied two different econometric models. The E3ME model predicts a slight increase in GDP (2–3 per cent) by 2050, while the GEM-E3 model suggests a small reduction of 1–2 per cent. But these are only minor variations in the context of a projected overall 85 per cent increase in GDP in the period 2013–50. Both models predict an increase in employment under various scenarios, up to 1.5 per cent. The largest increase is expected in the construction sector; power sector jobs could increase or decrease slightly; transport and energy-intensive manufacturing could lose jobs owing to higher energy costs; and jobs would be lost in the fossil fuel sector (including equipment manufacturing) (Cambridge Econometrics et al., 2013).

In the United States, a joint report by the Center for American Progress and the Political Economy Research Institute quantifies the level of investment required for the country to reduce its CO_2 emissions from energy-based sources by 40 per cent over the 20 years from 2015. The report concluded that investing about US$200 billion annually (US$110 billion in renewable energy, and the remaining US$90 billion in energy efficiency of buildings, transportation systems and industrial equipment) would reduce energy consumption by 30 per cent, cut CO_2 emissions from 5.6 billion tonnes in 2010 to 3 billion tonnes in 2030, and generate 4.2 million jobs (a 2.7 million net increase after taking into account a contraction in the fossil fuel sector). Net employment would expand at all levels of pay, and this investment package would lower the unemployment rate by 1.5 percentage points (Pollin et al., 2014).

Prospects in developing countries and emerging economies with little or no legacy of carbon- and resource-intensive infrastructure could be even better. These countries would reap the productivity and employment gains of twenty-first-century environmental technology without substitution effects.

2.1.2 Job quality and the upgrading of existing jobs

While a growing amount of analysis has been undertaken on the changes to the numbers of jobs in a greener economy, there is only limited evidence on the evolution of job quality.

The quality of indirect jobs in supply industries and of induced jobs from changed expenditure patterns and respending of savings from energy and resource efficiency is unlikely to change *per se* as a result of greening. Changes in job quality are mostly a function of the types of job created and lost.

Much of the additional employment in a greener economy will be created in the production of green goods and services. An assessment of a broad range of green jobs in the United States concludes that they compare favourably with non-green jobs in similar sectors in terms of higher skills levels and comparable or higher wages. Similarly, research in China, Germany and Spain has found the quality of new renewable energy jobs to be good. Data from Germany (Wissenschaftsladen Bonn, 2010) and Spain (Strietska-Ilina et al., 2011) indicate that renewables jobs are overwhelmingly permanent, full-time positions, with only a small share of temporary employment. In both countries, the renewables sector outperforms the economy as a whole in this regard. Studies in both countries also indicate that the qualification levels of workers in the renewable energy sector exceed the average for the national workforce by a substantial margin, in terms of both university degrees and vocational education and training levels (EC and ILO, 2011).

In China, too, workers at wind firms had higher average annual incomes and better job security, experienced better occupational conditions and enjoyed a higher level of workplace protection measures than their counterparts in conventional power plants. Some 77 per cent of Chinese wind power workers surveyed considered their work environment "very good", compared with just 18 per cent in large thermal power plants and 13 per cent in small plants (ILS and MOHRSS, 2010).

There is no question that switching from fossil fuels to renewables entails a vast improvement in the occupational health situation. This is especially true with regard to coalmining. Although the work tends to pay well, coalmining is one of the most hazardous industries for workers in terms of their long-term health and exposure to accidents (Summer and Layde, 2009). Some occupational hazards do of course exist in the renewables sector as well, such as potential exposure to a number of toxic substances in solar photovoltaic manufacturing, which requires proper safety and waste recovery procedures. Emerging thin-film and nanotech-based solar technologies may prompt new occupational concerns (SVTC, 2009, 2014). In the still young concentrated solar power industry, construction and maintenance of industrial-scale installations entails some electrical hazards, and hazards from concentrated sunlight in the form of potential exposure to high temperatures. For solar thermal equipment, installers who previously worked only on gas systems will face increased exposure to electrical work (EASHW, 2011).

As noted in Chapter 1, many of the jobs directly affected by environmental sustainability are in primary sectors of the economy such as agriculture, forestry and fishing. Others are in waste collection and recycling, or building construction. In many parts of the world, these sectors involve a large number of jobs that are low-paid, strenuous and/or dangerous. They typically offer little in the way of job security or social benefits, and a large proportion are in the informal economy.

A competent, skilled and motivated workforce is indispensable for better environmental performance. Without improvements in conditions, key sectors are unlikely to attract and retain a good calibre of worker. Across a number of economic sectors there is therefore a need and a significant opportunity for increasing the quality of work through improved working conditions, better OSH and higher incomes. Agriculture, waste management and recycling, and construction stand out in this regard,[3] albeit for

3   The following text is a condensed version of the analysis presented in the respective sector chapters of ILO and IILS (2012a). The reader is referred to these chapters for a more comprehensive consideration of the subject.

different reasons and with different options for achieving the necessary improvements.

2.1.2.1 Agriculture

In no other sector do the social and environmental challenges stand in greater contrast to one another. Even though its share has fallen over the last two decades, agriculture is still the largest employer in the world, with a global workforce of over 1 billion—about one in every three workers (ILO, 2012a). With agricultural incomes growing more slowly than GDP (World Bank, 2008), it is also the sector with the highest concentration of poor people, two-thirds of whom live in rural areas. Yet agriculture is one of the largest emitters of GHG and, very probably, the sector most vulnerable to climate change (IPCC, 2007). Moreover, it is the largest user (70 per cent), and a significant polluter, of water and a key cause of land degradation and loss of biodiversity (OECD, 2012a).

Despite these issues, an increase of up to 70 per cent in world food production from 2000 levels is needed to feed a growing population and provide a more resource-intensive diet. The evidence (UNEP, 2011c) suggests that these challenges can be met if there is a strong drive to train farmers, especially small-scale farmers in developing countries, in productive farming methods with a low environmental impact. Low-impact methods tend to be more labour-intensive, and therefore would allow agriculture to continue to absorb new workers in the short to medium term. These methods can also improve working conditions, in particular with regard to OSH. In particular, the responsible use and management of pesticides and other hazardous chemicals can make a major contribution to improved OSH as well as reduced environmental impact.

One of the most important policy measures to achieve this outcome, then, is to enhance the skills and capabilities of smallholder farmers in developing countries. To do this, investment in extension services will be required, and will need to be complemented by rural infrastructures and the development of the non-farm rural economy.

Successful outcomes will require a narrowing of the income gap between farm and non-farm households, which has widened over the past decades. Significantly higher incomes and poverty reduction can be achieved if output increases while production costs fall. Examples from Madagascar and India (ILO and IILS, 2012a, pp. 25, 28) and from Uganda (see box 2.1) show that substantial improvements can be achieved in a relatively short timeframe through improved farming methods and marketing. Over the longer

Box 2.1: Sustainable agriculture in Uganda

Agriculture is Uganda's major source of GDP and provides 69 per cent of all employment. The sector's output comes exclusively from about 4.5 million smallholder farmers, 80 per cent of whom own less than 2 hectares of land.

Uganda has undergone a significant process of land conversion in the past two decades, starting in 1994 when a few commercial companies chose to engage in organic agriculture. By 2003, a general movement towards developing sustainable agriculture as a means of improving people's livelihoods had turned Uganda's land area under organic agriculture production into the world's 13th largest, and the largest in Africa.

Since then, sustainable practices have continued to expand. In 2011 the country had 226,954 hectares under organic agricultural management (up from 210,245 hectares in 2008–09). The number of farmers certified organic rose from 180,746 to 187,893. Income improved as the farm-gate prices of organic pineapple, ginger and vanilla rose to levels 300, 185 and 150 per cent higher, respectively, than those of conventional products in 2006. Uganda's certified organic exports increased from US$3.7 million in 2003–04 to US$22.8 million in 2007–08.

Organic farming is also a low-carbon growth path. GHG emissions per hectare are estimated to be on average 64 per cent lower than emissions from conventional farms, as organic fields sequester 3–8 tonnes more carbon per hectare than conventionally cultivated fields.

Sources: Tumushabe et al. (2007); Namuwoza and Tushemerinwe (2011); UNCTAD and UNEP (2008); UNEP (2010b).

term, growing mechanization and an increase in the average size of farms are likely to be necessary to ensure that incomes in agriculture remain attractive relative to those in other sectors.

Employment guarantee schemes, as part of national social protection floors—in line with the ILO Social Protection Floors Recommendation, 2012 (No. 202)—can also play a major role in sheltering rural communities from crop failures, injecting finance into cash-starved rural areas and creating productive infrastructure. The Mahatma Gandhi National Rural Employment Guarantee Act (MGNREGA) in India (see box 2.2), for example, links direct income transfers through public works programmes on a large scale with investment in rural water management, irrigation, soil improvement and access to roads. Among several other programmes, Sampoorna Grameen Rojgar Yojana is also noteworthy as it seeks to shore up food security through employment (Govindan and Bhanot, 2012).

Solutions must be adapted to specific situations, built on the local farming system and developed in cooperation with the farming communities

Box 2.2: The Mahatma Gandhi National Rural Employment Guarantee Act, India (MGNREGA)

Devised as a public employment programme, MGNREGA provides at least 100 days of guaranteed waged employment per financial year to every rural household whose adult members volunteer to undertake unskilled manual work. Environmental protection and conservation, such as soil and water conservation, drought proofing (including reforestation), flood protection, small-scale irrigation and horticulture, and land development constitute the lion's share of work performed. In 2012/13, MGNREGA provided work to 50 million rural households at a cost of US$8.9 billion, up from 21 million beneficiary households in 2006–07.

Implementation has been uneven, depending on local capacity and commitment. There are many issues regarding the planning and technical quality of works, their integration into local development and governance. Critics note that one of MGNREGA's most important provisions—community-driven planning and prioritization of local needs—has not been pursued seriously, and many water conservation structures have not been completed. Also, the emphasis on creating as many unskilled positions as possible means that MGNREGA is missing an opportunity to contribute to skill building. There is also room for increasing the access for adult members of families who are, in principle, entitled to guaranteed work, and for improving working conditions and building pathways out of what is essentially a transfer scheme. MGNREGA is nevertheless clearly a big step in the right direction.

The Act represents a massive investment in the rehabilitation of natural capital related to poverty reduction. The programme has an economic as well as a social and environmental function, and is part of the broader sustainable development agenda which includes the National Action Plan on Climate Change (2008). An inter-ministerial task force deals with employment issues related to climate change, renewable energy and green jobs.

According to a study conducted by the Centre for Science and the Environment in 2009, the programme has managed most notably to increase water availability and improved agricultural production through better access to irrigation. This has led to greater crop diversity and enabled farmers to switch from single to dual crops. Similar programmes, albeit on a smaller scale, are also being implemented in South Africa.

Sources: UNDP (2010c); Lieuw-Kie-Song (2009); Harsdorff, Lieuw-Kie-Song and Tsukamoto (2011); ESID (2013); Mahapatra, Suchitra and Moyna (2011); Sanghi and Sharma (2014).

themselves. The organization of farmers and workers is an important stepping stone to giving rural communities a voice in policy-making for rural development and greening agriculture, with a particular emphasis on the inclusion of women farmers. Organization will also be critical for acquiring the capability to implement more productive, low-environmental-impact farming methods. The formation of cooperatives can help to spread access to know-how, inputs, finance and markets at fair prices, as illustrated by the experience of large cooperatives such as the Oromia Coffee Growers in Ethiopia, which is bringing substantial benefits to over 200,000 producers of organically grown coffee.[4] In Ghana, the objectives of the Kuapa Kokoo cooperative are to "empower small-scale cocoa producers, enhance female participation in the decision-making process, and encourage environmentally sustainable production". From just 200 members in 1993, Kuapa Kokoo grew to represent about 65,000 farmers by 2012, of which more than a quarter were women (Fairtrade Foundation, n.d.; Modern Ghana, 2012). In Costa Rica and India, cooperatives have become leaders in the production of carbon-neutral coffee and in using agricultural residues for power generation.

2.1.2.2 Waste management and recycling

In a world faced with escalating volumes of often hazardous waste, increased emphasis on recycling and waste management will be necessary to reduce pressure on natural resources and safeguard the environment. Mounting volumes of toxic, chemical, electronic or otherwise hazardous wastes are being shipped across countries and continents, moving from rich countries in the West to the poorest countries in, especially, South and South-East Asia and Africa. These exports are often illegal, violating national regulations as well as international agreements such as the 1989 Basel Convention on the Control of Transboundary Movements of Hazardous Wastes and their Disposal and the 2006 European Waste Shipment Regulation.

Stepping up recycling and reuse rates will create new employment, but the biggest challenge is upgrading informal to formal employment. This is necessary to cope with more complex recycling processes, to offer workers secure jobs with acceptable income levels, and to protect them from traditional and new hazards such as electronic waste.

The waste management and recycling industry is already a significant employer: an estimated 4 million workers are employed in the formal sector,[5] with another 15–20 million estimated to be working as informal waste-pickers in developing countries.[6] Although firm data are hard to come by, it is thought that a large percentage of workers involved in recycling and

4   For additional information, see ILO and IILS (2012a), p. 30.
5   Based on studies in China, Europe and the United States; see Tellus Institute (2011); FoE (UK) (2010).
6   Calculated on the basis of Bonner (2008).

waste management are women, often working as waste-pickers at the lower end of the informal economy.

Increased recycling can lead to significant gains in energy and employment. Specifically, recycling saves large amounts of energy when compared with the mining and processing of raw materials. Recycling aluminium, for example, offers savings of 95 per cent; the rates for steel (74 per cent) and paper (65 per cent) are also substantial (BIR, 2009).

Recycling can also lead to net gains in employment quantity and quality in comparison with traditional jobs in landfill or incineration of waste. US assessments have found that sorting and processing of recyclables sustains ten times as many jobs per tonne as landfill or incineration, a finding confirmed by a report from the United Kingdom. A study in India puts the recycling advantage as high as 24:1, while the European Environment Agency (EEA) concluded that recycling creates more jobs at higher incomes than landfilling or incinerating waste (ILSR, n.d.; FoE (UK), 2010; Alliance of Indian Wastepickers, 2010; EEA, 2011). The employment potential is particularly strong in countries whose recycling rates are currently low, as is the case in most developing countries and in Central and Eastern Europe.

Much greater quantities of recyclable materials are recovered by informal waste-pickers than by formal waste management companies. Informal pickers generate a net economic benefit for the municipalities where they work. However, informal recycling often involves hazardous working conditions for waste-pickers, many of whom live in poverty. Typically working without any kind of protective equipment, they are exposed to a range of toxins and to microbial or parasitic infections. The recovery of valuable metals from electronic waste is also often carried out in ways that endanger the pickers' health and safety. Moreover, waste increasingly contains hazardous chemicals and nano-materials.

Recycling will only become a truly green activity when it is formalized. In fact, organization of workers can turn waste management and recycling into a very significant opportunity for social inclusion and help improve working conditions, safety and health, and earnings, as demonstrated by experiences in cities around the world. One way to achieve this is for waste-picker cooperatives to be recognized by municipal authorities, as is demonstrated by a number of examples in Latin America, especially in Brazil and Colombia, as well as in Sri Lanka (see box 2.3) (Bonner, 2008; Khullar, 2009; AVINA, 2009, 2010). Indeed, working with community and waste-picker organizations is infinitely preferable to trying to sideline them through ill-conceived privatization efforts.

Box 2.3: Upgrading recycling work in Brazil and Sri Lanka

Brazil

Brazil has the world's largest national waste-pickers' movement. The income of its some 60,000 members is three to five times higher than that of unorganized waste-pickers. This is the fruit of an effective mix of policies put in place by the Brazilian Government over the past decade. Policies include legal recognition, entrepreneurial development, municipal government contracts and facilities (sorting stations), modern recycling methods, skills development, and OSH precautions, as well as measures to prevent and discourage child labour. These measures have triggered large-scale improvements in recycling efficiency, working conditions and incomes. The Brazilian poverty eradication strategy *Brasil Sem Miséria*, launched by President Rousseff in June 2011, aims to scale up this approach and formalize a further 250,000 waste-pickers in addition to those already organized.

Sri Lanka

Sri Lanka has initiated a strategy to improve working conditions and the formalization of jobs among the most vulnerable categories of informal workers, including those in waste management. A total of 4,000 waste-handlers, truck drivers, waste-sorters/collectors and local communities across seven zones in the Western Province have been made aware of the importance of OSH at work. OSH standards have been integrated into the National Vocational Qualification certification for waste management operations, endorsed by the national Tertiary and Vocational Education Commission (TVEC). The national OSH Act was expanded to the workplaces and workers involved in waste management. The Waste Management Authority agreed to trade unions providing training to workers on collective bargaining and labour issues.

Sources: Brazil: Dias (2011); Dias and Alves (2008); Sri Lanka: ILO (2012c).

2.1.2.3 Buildings and construction

Buildings are the single largest consumer of energy and the largest emitter of GHGs. Yet the building sector also has the highest potential for improving energy efficiency and reducing emissions. Experience in a growing number of countries, both industrialized and developing, demonstrates that the construction of energy- and resource-efficient buildings requires competent enterprises and a skilled workforce.

Many investments in energy- and water-efficient buildings are cost-effective. The large stocks of older and inefficient buildings, notably in industrialized countries, mean that greater emphasis on renovation could yield substantial environmental benefits. For emerging economies and developing countries, leapfrogging directly to high-performance new buildings will avoid a legacy of high energy, water and resource consumption which otherwise would endure for decades.

Poorly installed equipment and materials do not yield expected gains in efficiency and emissions reduction, as a study from California shows. Worker training is part of the remedy, but must be accompanied by efforts to overcome market conditions that lead many employers to compete on the basis of cost rather than quality, along with better enforcement of building permits, codes and standards (IRLE, 2011; Mattera et al., 2009). Skills upgrading and redesigning of work methods will also be needed to overcome traditional OSH hazards such as asbestos, a legacy which needs to be dealt with in building renovation, and to prevent possible new hazards associated with new construction materials and methods.

In Gaza an ILO study (ILO, 2012d) on reconstruction works and low-cost housing showed that significant economic, employment and environmental gains can be made by using compressed earth blocks and other recycled building material as an alternative to cement. Gains are also made through the sustainable use of existing water resources and the reuse of sewage water, as well as by introducing energy efficiency measures and using renewable energy sources such as solar and wind. Yet these gains can only be realized if the shift towards green construction is accompanied by skills development strategies that address the skills gaps at all levels of occupation.

Targeted investments in skills upgrading and certification of building firms, formalization (notably of SMEs, which dominate the sector) and improvements in working conditions to retain qualified workers are essential components of a successful strategy.

There are at least 110 million formal sector construction workers employed worldwide, and an unknown number of labourers working in informal jobs with generally poor working conditions. Even jobs in the formal construction sector are among the most hazardous forms of employment in terms of work accidents and occupational diseases. Jobs are also often temporary, with complex subcontracting arrangements. In most countries, the construction workforce has high proportions of low-skilled workers and of migrant workers.

The renovation of existing and the construction of new energy-efficient buildings represent large potential employment benefits. Jobs are created not only in the construction sector, but also in industries that produce insulation and other energy efficiency materials, as well as in the growing energy services sector (Syndex, S. Partner and WMP, 2009; ILO, 2011c; Trabish,

2011). A policy mix of building standards, credit and incentives, along with a role for intermediaries such as energy service companies, can boost green building renovation activity, with public finance mobilizing ("crowding in") private investment.

Retrofitting investments can have a strong immediate effect on employment generation in the construction sector and its suppliers. Moreover, savings from improved efficiency will be channelled back into the economy with important multiplier effects on economic activity, employment creation and income generation. The International Energy Agency (IEA)'s *World Energy Outlook*, for example, estimates that a US$2.5 trillion additional investment in green buildings globally between 2010 and 2030 would yield US$5 trillion in energy savings over the life of the investment (IEA, 2009).

The large-scale renovation programme for energy efficiency in Germany, for example, has mobilized investments of €118 billion since 2006. In 2010, the programme helped to create or maintain some 340,000 jobs in the building industry. The programme is also notable for the fact that it was initiated jointly by trade unions, employers and non-governmental organizations (NGOs)—a cooperative model rooted in social dialogue (Government of Germany, n.d.). A US study found that energy efficiency retrofits of pre-1980 building stock could reduce electricity use by 30 per cent and create more than 3.3 million cumulative job-years of employment (Deutsche Bank Climate Change Advisors and Rockefeller Foundation, 2012). A longer-term (2011–50) assessment of the impacts of the EU's 2010 Energy Performance of

Box 2.4: The employment benefits of green retrofitting in Hungary

A recent study undertaken by Ürge-Vorsatz et al. looking at the net employment impacts of a large-scale energy efficiency renovation programme in Hungary simulates five scenarios, including a "deep retrofit, fast implementation rate" scenario which assumes that 5.7 per cent of the total floor area will be renovated per year.

A renovation programme of this scale could generate up to 131,000 net jobs in the country, whereas a less ambitious scenario would see the creation of only about 43,000 new jobs. Under the "deep renovation" scenario, job creation would peak in 2015 with a massive 184,000 new jobs, notwithstanding employment losses in the energy supply sector. It is important to highlight that almost 38 per cent of these employment gains derive from indirect effects on sectors supplying the construction sector, as well as from the higher spending power resulting from the previous rise in employment.

Source: Ürge-Vorsatz et al. (2010).

Buildings Directive concluded that an accelerated pace of renovation could generate an average of 0.5 million to 1.1 million jobs per annum (Buildings Performance Institute Europe, 2011). Box 2.4 illustrates the potential in the case of Hungary.

Energy- and resource-efficient social housing has the potential to improve living standards and shield poor households from rising energy prices, while avoiding costly investments in power generation capacity. This is demonstrated by the Brazilian programme "Minha Casa, Minha Vida" (My Home, My Life) for low-income families, which aims to equip 300,000 houses with solar water heaters, saving families 40 per cent on their energy bills (see also box 3.7). The programme is expected to create 30,000 additional skilled jobs related to the manufacturing and installation of the equipment (ECLAC and ILO, 2010; Café, 2011). Energy access can also have wider employment and income benefits.

2.1.3 Contributing to social inclusion

Chapter 1 pointed out that the poor are disproportionately affected by the deterioration of the natural environment, as evident in pollution, biodiversity loss or the impact of climate change. While their income is heavily skewed towards direct dependence on natural resources, a much higher share of the expenditure of poor households goes on energy (direct as well as embedded energy such as food and transport) than among wealthier households. The situation is aggravated by the fact that many poor households have no access to energy-efficient housing or transport.

However, with the right investment and policy conditions, the transformation to environmental sustainability offers the possibility of greater social inclusion, including better opportunities for women and thus contributing to gender equality. New services and related employment opportunities can become available for people hitherto excluded or disfavoured in the labour market. Two ways in which this is starting to happen are access to clean energy and payment for environmental services.

2.1.3.1 Energy access

Some 1.3 billion people in developing countries have no access to clean modern energy at all and 2.7 billion do not have clean and safe cooking facilities (UN, 2012). On current trends of extending access, some 15 per cent of the world population would still be without access in 2030, the majority of them in sub-Saharan Africa (IEA, UNDP and UNIDO, 2010). Greater efforts to promote income security and affordable renewable energy can make a major contribution to overcoming energy poverty and the lack of access to energy. Moreover, they can also create badly needed employment and income opportunities in the production of energy and even more so through the use of that energy. The use of electricity in particular has enormous potential to improve productivity. As pointed out in a revealing recent study shedding new light on the historic drivers of economic productivity, the highest increases sustained over the longest period have been associated with the introduction of electricity, sanitation and running water (Gordon, 2012).

A programme in Bangladesh initiated by the NGO Grameen Shakti and further scaled up with support from the Bureau of Manpower, Employment and Training demonstrates the benefits, and how access to clean energy can be achieved on a large scale (see box 2.5).

Box 2.5: Solar home systems (SHS) in Bangladesh

Approximately half of the population of Bangladesh—some 85 million people—lacks access to grid-based electricity. The government issued a roadmap in 2010 to extend electrification to all Bangladeshis. Since 2003, installations of SHS have grown rapidly, reaching 3.3 million units by October 2014, and expanding at a monthly rate of about 70,000. The goal is to reach 6 million units by 2016. A rapidly rising number of people, currently estimated at 14 million, have gained access to electricity. The driving force behind these efforts has been Grameen Shakti, a subsidiary of microcredit pioneer Grameen Bank. A number of multilateral and bilateral donors have supported this effort, and the government signed an agreement with the World Bank in June 2014 for US$78.4 million in financing for 480,000 additional units.

SHS offer a light source that is far more powerful than highly polluting kerosene lamps, and provide battery power for mobile phones, radios and televisions. The power output facilitates the growth of small businesses providing services such as mobile phone charging, and increases the hours during which children can study for school.

Project partners working with the Infrastructure Development Company Ltd (IDCOL), established by the government to finance infrastructure and renewable energy projects, employ an estimated 70,000 people. According to Dipal Barua of the Bright Green Energy Foundation, another 10,000–15,000 people work in SHS projects separate from IDCOL, and 30,000 more find employment in solar panel manufacturing and assembly. Altogether, as many as 115,000 people gain incomes from the solar programme. The introduction of SHS requires a range of skills and occupations, including solar energy technicians, service engineers, branch managers and financial specialists. Most of the workers are young "field assistants" who sell and install SHS, and provide maintenance services. Technical training programmes at about 50 Green Technology Centres have benefited several thousand people.

Women have been major beneficiaries. Some 5,000 women have been instructed in the proper usage of SHS, and more than 1,000 female technicians trained to assemble, install and maintain them; the Green Technology Centres are run by female engineers.

Given the high priority the Government of Bangladesh has accorded to renewable energy sources,[7] the Bureau of Manpower, Employment and Training and the ILO, in collaboration with IDCOL, are working in partnership with Grameen Shakti to scale up and standardize skill acquisition among solar technicians and entrepreneurs. Competency-based training courses have been developed and delivered. Curricula, competency standards and occupational profiles are built into the country's National Technical and Vocational Qualification Framework. Trainees will thus have the opportunity to have their skills and competencies assessed and obtain a national certificate under the framework.

Sources: Strietska-Ilina et al. (2011); Barua (2014); IDCOL (n.d.); Haque (2014); World Bank (2014a); Bimes-doerfer, Kantz and Siegel (2011); Arthur (2010); UNCTAD (2009).

The example of Bangladesh shows that a greener economy can contribute to greater gender equality. Women would be the main beneficiaries from improvements in smallholder agriculture and in recycling, for example. Access to clean energy, to energy-efficient social housing and to affordable public transport would all alleviate current social burdens on women and open up new opportunities. However, broader and deeply rooted constraints on the greater involvement of women in the green economy, and their proportionate benefit, may well persist in some contexts. This point is further discussed in Chapter 4.

Tunisia's Solar Programme (PROSOL) is another encouraging story, providing more than 50,000 families with solar hot water services to date. Over 1,000 enterprises have entered the solar installation business, creating substantial numbers of jobs. The early success prompted the government to increase the target area for installed surface by nearly 100 per cent to 750,000 square metres in 2010–14 (UNEP, 2010b).

Energy access can also be enhanced by mobilizing social organizations such as cooperatives, as is apparent from examples in a growing number

7   The National Renewable Energy Policy, 2008 sets a target for renewable energy resources to meet 10 per cent of the national demand for electricity by 2020.

of countries including Argentina, Cambodia, Germany, India, Mexico and (with a long tradition) the United States (see also box 3.8).

The Sustainable Energy for All Initiative launched by the UN Secretary-General at the Rio+20 Conference aims to ensure universal access to modern energy services, doubling the global rate of improvement in energy efficiency and doubling the share of renewable energy in the global energy mix by 2030. Wider initiatives to enhance income security, for example by building national social protection floors, can also help to promote access to energy.

2.1.3.2 Payment for environmental services

Environmental services have significant economic benefits, often way beyond the locations and the communities where they are produced. Protecting forests in mountainous areas, for example, produces clean water and shelters downstream settlements and infrastructure from floods and landslides. Preserving tropical rainforests makes a major contribution to maintaining global biodiversity and to restricting GHG emissions. While the benefits accrue to downstream communities or even the world population at large, local communities incur the direct or the opportunity cost for providing the service. The rural and coastal populations concerned are often among the poorest in the country. Programmes operating as part of

---

Box 2.6: Green grants in Brazil

The "Bolsa Verde" (Green Grant) programme in Brazil compensates poor families affected by policies to reduce deforestation. The programme provides cash transfers of US$120 every three months for two years, conditional on families' commitments to maintain forest cover and engage in sustainable production activities. It supplements the national "Fome Zero" (Zero Hunger) and "Bolsa Família" (Family Allowance) programmes which provide income support to poor households generally.

The Bolsa Verde was introduced as part of the president's strategy for poverty eradication. From 3,286 in late 2011, the number of families included in Bolsa Verde rose to 69,126 by late 2014. Priority is given to women, who represent 88 per cent of beneficiaries. There are plans to extend the coverage to 300,000 families, encompassing a broader range of measures, such as clean energy use. (By comparison, the broader Bolsa Família social protection programme covered 14.1 million families in 2014.)

Source: Muchagata (2014).

Box 2.7: Green public employment schemes in South Africa

The Extended Public Works Programme (EPWP) in South Africa pursues a mix of poverty reduction and community-led development objectives through investments in economic, social and environmental infrastructure. Acknowledging that unemployment is caused by structural rather than cyclical problems, the EPWP was launched in 2004. Between the programme's first and third phases, the goal was raised from 1 million to 6 million work opportunities (these are not full-time equivalents (FTEs), however). Of the 6 million employment opportunities across the economy, the "environment and culture sector" accounts for 1.15 million.

The environmental scheme "Working for Water" improves water management through the removal of invasive alien vegetation; it created the equivalent of about 20,000 FTE jobs as of 2014. Other schemes contributing to providing jobs to vulnerable groups and local communities involve wetland and forest rehabilitation, fire management, renewable energy production, and eco-furniture. "Working for Wetlands" rehabilitated 906 wetlands with an area of more than 70,000 hectares, providing 12,848 employment opportunities and 168,400 days of skills training by 2013. With a total budget of 1.9 billion rand (ZAR), the various programmes generated close to 24,000 FTE jobs by 2012. By 2025, it is projected that 573 billion rand will be required to generate more than 230,000 FTE jobs.

Better monitoring and evaluation of impacts, and of services and assets created in poor communities, is needed. The government is planning to continue strong collaboration with the National Skills Fund and Skills Education and Training Agencies; where possible, EPWP beneficiaries will be moved into formal employment through cooperatives and small enterprise development.

or linked to national social protection floors are proving to be a powerful mechanism to link environmental and social objectives.

Payments to such communities are often necessary in order to enable them to continue rendering the services provided. Private companies as well as governments have begun to establish arrangements with local communities.[8] Government schemes on a large scale include payments to farmers in Costa Rica (Ortiz Malavasi, Sage Mora and Carvajal, 2003) and in the EU, the MGNREGA programme in India (see box 2.6), the "Bolsa Verde" programme in Brazil (see box 2.2), the Extended Public Works Programme (EPWP) in South Africa (see box 2.7). In Indonesia, community contracts have been a very successful mode of implementation in the Rural Access

---

8   For examples from Africa and Nicaragua, see ILO and IILS (2012a), pp. 44, 45.

	Number of FTE jobs			
	2012	2017	2025	
Working for Water	15,416	42,979	111,632	
Working for Energy (Biomass)	–	14,293	38,480	
Working for Land	3,485	23,941	63,749	
Working for Wetlands	1,775	7,051	9,921	
Working on Fire	3,239	7,042	7,042	
Total	23,915	95,306	230,824	

TABLE 2.1 Green jobs opportunities through South Africa's "Working for ..." programmes

Source: Preston (2014).

In addition to the EPWP, South Africa's Department of Environmental Affairs launched a number of green jobs projects, including "Groen Sebenza" (aimed at bridging the gap between education and job opportunities in the biodiversity sector, involving the placement of 800 unemployed young people for a period of two-and-a-half years), and the "Youth Jobs in Waste" programme (aiming to create job opportunities, on-the-job training and continuous upskilling, as well as small enterprise development, in the provinces of Free State and North West).

Sources: ILO (2010a); Nzimakwe (2008); Education and Training Unit (n.d.); South African Department of Environmental Affairs (n.d.); SANBI (n.d.); South African Department of Public Works (2014); South African Department of Environmental Affairs (2014).

and Capacity Building Project in Nias, which is part of the government's Reconstruction Continuation Plan.

One of the most promising global payment schemes involving international transfers from industrialized to developing countries is Reduced Emissions from Deforestation and Forest Degradation (REDD+) under the UNFCCC. The initiative goes beyond avoiding deforestation and forest degradation to emphasize the vital role of forest conservation, sustainable management of forests and enhancement of forest carbon sinks in reducing emissions. REDD+ can also become a vehicle for "ensuring a just transition of the workforce that creates decent work and quality jobs", as set out in the "shared vision" under the UNFCCC Cancún Agreements (UNFCCC, 2011, para. I:10). Directing investments towards labour-intensive value-added activities, such as ecosystem restoration, and thus generating employment for forest communities, is one of the most important strategies for REDD+. One recent example is the Indonesian Government's effort to enhance green livelihoods for local communities of Central Kalimantan, which will improve access to sustainable livelihoods through employment-intensive environmental infrastructure investments that adapt to climate change using participatory local resource-based approaches.

Currently, there are 56 partner developing countries registered in the UN-REDD programme, 21 of which are receiving support for their national programme activities. By March 2012, a total of US$67.8 million had been approved by the Policy Board for National Programmes (UN-REDD, n.d.). Financial flows are predicted to reach US$30 billion per year. This level of investment could sustain up to 8 million additional full-time workers in developing countries. Norway has pledged US$2.5 billion for REDD programmes. Large amounts of additional funding are flowing through voluntary carbon offset programmes, the World Bank Climate Investment Funds (US$5.7 billion) and the Global Environmental Facility (over US$28 billion).[9]

2.2 Lessons learned

The studies and experiences reviewed in this chapter represent a diverse range of countries and approaches, with analyses relying on a variety of different methods. In spite of this diversity, they appear to converge on a number of important results:

- In most cases, significant job creation potential exists and considerable net gains are possible. These are mostly in the range of 0.5–2 per cent of total employment, even in advanced economies with high substitution effects.

- The most pessimistic findings are that net employment gains or losses in the countries concerned would be so insignificant as to be neutral. Even this outcome would give countries the benefit of reduced environmental impacts and their attendant social cost. For the labour market it would mean no increase in the number of jobs, but more sustainable employment with higher job security and fewer negative externalities.

9   See http://www.climatefundsupdate.org.

- Policies matter: labour market impacts are largely a function of the policies applied. This message is consistently borne out by modelling and by practical experiences with transforming economies for environmental sustainability. Neither the number and quality of jobs created nor the net balance for employment come about automatically. Policy coherence often requires coordination across sectoral policy lines in areas including environment, infrastructure, housing, energy, agriculture and rural development, social protection and employment.

- Two important strands emerge in policy analysis: redistribution of cost and redistribution of investment. The first focuses on the way the transition cost imposed by prices put on emissions and resource consumption is absorbed by the economy. Environmental tax reform or eco-taxes, recycling revenue from environmental taxation to reduce the cost of labour, are a powerful tool to achieve coherence between economic, environmental and social outcomes.

- The second strand emphasizes the possibility of mobilizing additional investment through ambitious environmental policies. Combining this approach with eco-taxes could lead to significantly larger net gains in employment, while still reducing environmental footprints.

- The review of country evidence at the beginning of this chapter demonstrated that the location and extent of green jobs and broader employment potential depend on the structure of national economies, including their sectoral composition.

- The significance of green jobs goes beyond the creation of employment. They are not merely the passive outcome of redirecting investments into greening the economy. Rather, competent enterprises with skilled, motivated and enabled workers are critical for reaping the positive environmental and economic outcomes from the investments.

- The potential, and indeed the necessity, to upgrade existing jobs for better environmental and social outcomes exists in agriculture and recycling, where significant progress could be made in poverty reduction and social inclusion, and in the building sector in all countries.

- This will in many instances require initiatives to upgrade the competencies of enterprises and the job quality of workers as well as of their jobs. There are major opportunities to reduce exposure to traditional OSH hazards and to prevent the emergence of new ones.

- Finally, wider policies can help to enhance access to energy and promote environmentally sensitive livelihoods. In particular, social protection measures as part of social protection floors can be an effective mechanism to link environmental sustainability with social inclusion on a very large scale. Income transfers and public employment schemes, as well as social housing, can compensate poor households for the environmental services they render, and enhance access to energy and economic opportunity for vulnerable groups.

3

Identifying and managing the challenges

The risks and challenges for labour markets and social inclusion associated with the transition to environmentally sustainable development fall into three categories:

1. Economic restructuring

2. Climate change and the associated threat to jobs and livelihoods

3. Adverse income distribution effects originating from energy poverty

After examining the available evidence concerning the nature and extent of the challenges, this chapter reviews a number of country and sector experiences with policy responses to ensure smooth and just transitions for enterprises, workers and communities.

Although experience to date underscores the size and nature of the challenge, it has also revealed that the labour market and social outcomes are not givens, but are heavily conditioned by the policies applied. In all the cases that follow, policy approaches that integrate the three dimensions of sustainable development and make use of the inseparable and complementary nature of productive employment, social protection, labour rights and social dialogue are effective in ensuring a smooth and just transition which seizes the opportunities and minimizes the social and economic costs.

3.1 Economic restructuring

3.1.1 Nature and scope of the adjustments needed

Economic restructuring and related shifts in labour markets driven by environmental factors can be economy-wide or concentrated in certain sectors, regions and communities. They are generally permanent, but there are also instances of important temporary adjustments.

The sectors most directly concerned by such adjustments are resource- and energy-intensive industries, which are also major sources of pollution and emissions; and primary industries, such as forestry and fisheries, when they overuse the natural resources on which they depend. Restructuring in resource-intensive industries most strongly affects industrialized countries and some emerging economies. China, for example, estimates that its national energy efficiency and pollution reduction policies will lead to the loss of over 800,000 jobs in obsolete power-generation and steel-making plants in the period 2005–20 (CASS, 2010).

3.1.1.1 The largest polluters represent a modest share of total employment So what are the losses to be expected? The evidence available to date suggests that losses in aggregate employment from environmental policies are less than one might think. One reason is the relatively modest share of total employment in the 10–15 industries which have the greatest environmental impact. In OECD countries, the seven most polluting industries account for over 80 per cent of total emissions while employing only about 10 per cent of the workforce, albeit in mostly well-paid jobs (for the comparable situation in the EU, see figure 3.1). ILO estimates for a wider range of countries arrive at similar proportions. Table 3.1 shows that energy production and

TABLE 3.1   Global employment in resource-intensive sectors

Sector/industry	Employment (millions)
Extraction of oil and gas	3
Coalmining[1]	7
Utilities (including water)[2]	11
Energy-intensive manufacturing[3]	11
Electric and electronic products[3]	18
Total	**50**

Sources: [1] World Coal Institute (2005). [2] ILO (2011d). [3] UNEP (2011c).

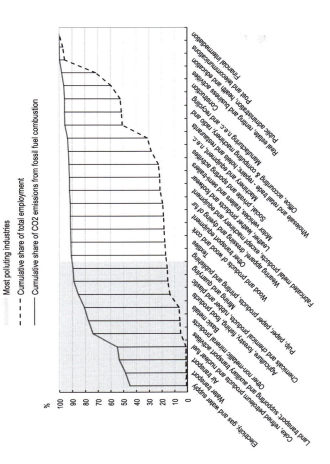

FIGURE 3.1   CO$_2$ emissions and employment, EU-25, 2005

Note: n.e.c. = not elsewhere counted.

Source: ILO and OECD (2012).

some of the most energy- and resource-intensive sectors employ only about 50 million workers worldwide in a global workforce of over 3 billion.

The share of employment in resource-intensive sectors tends to be higher in countries with lower GDP per capita and can be substantially higher in individual countries irrespective of the level of national income. As yet, research findings are lacking on potential impacts in such countries.

3.1.1.2 Greening is often a relatively minor factor in employment losses

Closer inspection also shows that environmental and resource issues are only one factor leading to job losses. Evidence reviewed in the ILO/IILS report suggests that greening has so far been a minor factor in any reduction in employment (ILO and IILS, 2012a). In fact, the principal causes of declining employment in industries such as mining, fossil energy or iron and steel have been the increasing automation and rising labour productivity that have been occurring over several decades.

In most countries, employment in power plants has declined over the past two decades, following deregulation and growing automation. Some 70,000 South African power sector jobs were lost between 1980 and 2000, at the same time as electricity generation increased by more than 60 per cent. In the EU, an estimated 300,000 jobs in the electricity generation sector were cut between 1997 and 2004 (GCN, 2010).

As the most carbon-intensive fuel producer, the coal industry will probably feel the shock of a transition to greater sustainability more than any other sector. Even without curbs in production China has cut its workforce in coalmining by half, with an estimated 3.8 million coalminers in 2009 down from 7.6 million in 1992 (Qingyi, 2010). In the United States, too, growing automation and labour productivity have led to a steep drop in coalmining employment, from 785,000 miners in 1920 to a low of 69,000 in 2003, though recovering to 87,000 in 2011. In 2014, about 78,000 coalminers were employed (SourceWatch, 2011; USBLS, n.d.).

The growth of the renewable energy industry has to date actually supplemented jobs in the fossil fuel sector, rather than replaced them. This may change if GHG emissions are cut as strongly as called for by climate science. Unless technologies such as carbon capture and storage, which would neutralize emissions from fossil fuels, become technically and economically viable, absolute reductions in fossil energy use would precipitate job losses in these industries.

Nonetheless, the overall extent of restructuring may be smaller than some have expected, at least when considering the impact of reducing GHG emissions to levels in line with the international target of limiting global warming to a maximum of 2°C.

3.1.1.3 Climate change mitigation policies mainly affect sectoral employment composition

The OECD has recently made use of its global ENV-Linkages computable general equilibrium model referred to in Chapter 2 to analyse how ambitious climate change mitigation policies could affect labour market outcomes (ILO and IILS, 2012a). These simulations show that a well-designed emissions trading system could achieve sharp reductions in GHG emissions while only moderately slowing GDP growth in the coming decades. The main labour market impacts of the mitigation policies will be to alter the sectoral composition of employment, with fossil fuel industries experiencing the steepest declines and renewable energy industries the sharpest increases (see figure 3.2).

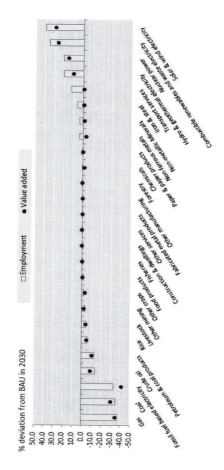

FIGURE 3.2   Simulated changes in sectoral composition of employment associated with an ambitious climate change mitigation policy, OECD countries

Source: Chateau, Saint-Martin and Manfredi (2011).

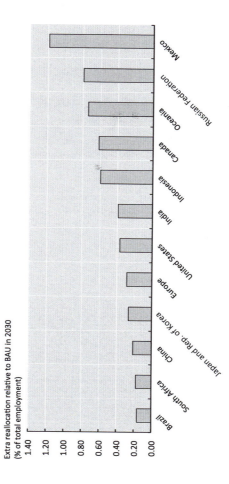

FIGURE 3.3   Simulated increase in relocation, by country

Source: Chateau, Saint-Martin and Manfredi (2011).

On the whole, restructuring would lead to less than 1 per cent of all workers having to change to another economic sector. While earlier experience with restructuring suggests that the number of workers changing enterprises would be larger than those changing sectors, the shifts induced by climate change policies would be much smaller than the 20 per cent job reallocation OECD countries have experienced over the last two decades as a result of globalization (Chateau, Saint-Martin and Manfredi, 2011). In keeping with other findings on major differences between countries, the modelling shows that the intensity of the induced job reallocation varies significantly across G20 countries. Energy exporters would see the largest shifts (figure 3.3).

OECD and earlier ILO modelling also illustrates how the functioning of the labour market itself could affect the overall cost of sharply reducing GHG emissions. If labour markets adapt smoothly, the impact of mitigation policy on GDP growth is small. This finding illustrates the importance of combining ambitious environmental policies with measures to lower the cost of labour through eco-taxes, and support to increase the adaptive capacity of labour markets for strong employment performance.

In conclusion, while losses in energy-intensive sectors are likely, large losses are not inevitable. In addition to policy instruments such as an eco-tax, other effects and measures can contain the drop in overall employment. According to ILO studies, even resource- and energy-intensive sectors could see an employment gain while energy use and emissions fall. The increase in energy cost would lead to cleaner products and processes, while reductions in the cost of labour would avoid an overall increase in the cost of products which would otherwise result in lost market share and output. Reduced labour costs would be sufficient to increase employment per unit output in energy-intensive sectors (ILO and IILS, 2009, ch. 4).

3.1.2 Getting the best employment outcomes from greening enterprises and supply chains

3.1.2.1 Greening enterprises: raising resource productivity is key

Many resource-intensive industries have two important characteristics that influence employment in a restructuring process:

1. They can benefit from increased demand in green growth sectors to which they supply important inputs.

2. They are sensitive to price signals related to resource scarcity and environmental policy measures.

Improving energy and materials productivities is therefore one important means of securing the future viability of these industries and their workforces.

This is, in fact, already happening. A survey of US manufacturing by the US Bureau of Labor Statistics (USBLS), for example, found that almost 100,000 jobs—out of a total of about 700,000 jobs in four basic industries—can be considered green because they produce green goods and services. The largest share is found in the steel sector (USBLS, 2012).

Greening measures protect existing jobs and in some cases can actually boost employment considerably. One example is the recycling of the large amounts of heat produced by basic industries. Using the employment per gigawatt (GW) of combined heat and power (CHP) found dissipated in the United States, the global CHP capacity of 330 GW could provide more than 820,000 jobs at new CHP facilities (Munson, 2009). Direct jobs are complemented by indirect employment at supplier companies, site developers, firms involved in designing, constructing and installing CHP facilities and related equipment, and those in energy efficiency consulting. CHP promises a win–win solution for manufacturing industries. In the United States, a large-scale expansion of CHP could provide 20 per cent of electricity generating capacity by 2030 and create nearly 1 million highly skilled jobs (Recycled Energy Development, 2010). The IEA offers a projection of CHP potential by 2030 for the G8 + 5 countries[1] of 833 GW, or about 500 GW more than today (IEA, 2008). Disregarding improvements in labour productivity, the same rough formula would suggest a global employment potential of more than 2 million jobs.

Green manufacturing can act as a catalyst for life-cycle innovation and green job creation—as well as job retention—in the manufacturing sector and its value chains, including services for product ecodesign, industrial ecology, energy efficiency and renewable energy, waste management and valuation of natural assets. The greening of manufacturing can lead to significant reductions in resource use and pollution in these energy-intensive industries and help to save existing jobs by improving overall efficiency and generating new revenue from former waste materials and energy.

3.1.2.2 Getting employees and the social partners involved

Successful drives to green resource-intensive industries have been made by individual companies as well as by entire sectors. The social partners have often played an important role. The highly successful case of the workplace cooperation at the large global manufacturer 3M is described in box 3.1.

Another example is the electronics company LG Electronics of the Republic of Korea, which has also actively encouraged its employees to

1   The G8 + 5 are: Canada, France, Germany, Italy, Japan, Russian Federation, United Kingdom and United States plus Brazil, China, India, Mexico and South Africa.

Box 3.1: Higher resource efficiency in enterprises—the example of 3M

The conglomerate 3M has applied an integrated strategy to improve the company's resource use, measuring and tracking progress of the business benefits and engaging employees to ensure continual improvement. 3M had reduced its worldwide GHG emissions by 72 per cent in 2011 from a 1990 baseline, and emissions of volatile organic compounds by 95 per cent.

The company's "Pollution Prevention Pays" (3P) programme, initiated in 1975, has cumulatively prevented the production of more than 1.4 billion kilograms of pollutants and saved the company US$1.4 billion.

The 3P programme depends directly on the voluntary participation of 3M employees, who have completed over 8,600 3P projects to date. Projects must meet criteria such as reducing energy use, making more efficient use of materials and resources, and saving money (for example, through reduced operating and materials expenses and increased sales of products).

The company's 2015 Sustainability Goals include targets to reduce waste by 10 per cent by 2015 from a 2010 base year, and to improve energy efficiency by 25 per cent by 2015 from a 2005 base year. 3M is also planning to review suppliers in Brazil, China, India, Malaysia, Mexico, the Republic of Korea, Russian Federation, Taiwan (China), China, Thailand and Turkey, to ensure compliance with its environmental, health and safety, transportation, labour and human relations standards by 2015.

Source: 3M (2011).

engage in such efforts (LG Electronics, 2011). It recently established a global labour policy, defining a baseline for over 120 work sites and offices worldwide. Its LGE Labour Union has issued a Union Social Responsibility Charter and established an action plan covering seven core subject areas, including governance, labour and environment (advancing a "low-carbon culture"). By 2010, the company claimed that GHG emissions from its manufacturing operations were 160,000 tonnes below the 2008 level, and that GHG emissions from the use of its products were 12.75 million tonnes lower than would have been the case in the absence of efficiency measures. Over 20,000 employees based in China, Europe and North America participated in its online climate change training in 2010/11.

An innovative example of a policy designed to promote efficiency standards for a whole sector is Japan's "Top Runner" programme for electrical appliances in buildings and transport. Instead of setting a minimum efficiency standard, the most efficient model on the market is identified and others have to match it within four to eight years. This provides time for manufacturers to adapt and/or invent an even more efficient product. The

Top Runner standards are set by committees comprising representatives from manufacturing industry, trade unions, universities and consumer organizations.

Such initiatives in greening enterprises play a vital role not only in reducing environmental impact, but also in improving competitiveness and securing existing employment in resource-intensive sectors. The main opportunities, and the labour market implications, do not necessarily lie within the enterprise itself. They may be found along the supply chain of inputs or extend to the downstream marketing, use and disposal of products. Environmental and social life-cycle assessments can be a very useful tool for identifying opportunities for improvement. Guidelines have been issued by UNEP in 2009 and applied, for example, to the ICT sector (UNEP and SETC, 2009; Ciroth and Franze, 2011).

3.1.2.3 Small businesses face specific challenges in going green

An important dimension of greening enterprises is the role of SMEs, which represent the vast majority of all enterprises, accounting for more than two-thirds of all permanent employment (Ayyagari, Demirguc-Kunt and Maksimovic, 2011). They are also the largest source of new job creation and innovation. While most SMEs are low-risk installations and the environmental footprint of the individual SME is typically small, collectively they are significant polluters and consumers of resources. As such, their role will determine how successful the transformation to a green economy will be, both in terms of environmental sustainability and as regards employment and income distribution. The creation and growth of SMEs depends particularly strongly on access to information, to understanding of green markets, and to skills programmes, technologies and finance.

Larger firms have better access to information, internal human resources, financial resources and technology than most SMEs. A study of 15 enterprises in different European countries documents the success of larger firms in tackling the demands of environmental sustainability (GHK Consulting, 2009). SMEs, on the other hand, face many challenges in this respect (De Gobbi, 2011). They face far greater difficulties in compensating for rising energy and raw material costs by improving processes and technology and in absorbing new environmental standards imposed by legislators and consumers. They also miss out more easily on the major business opportunities arising in green markets. This puts SMEs at an added disadvantage and carries the risk of inadvertent structural change, which would jeopardize employment creation.

Despite these challenges, SMEs can and should become sustainable enterprises that combine the legitimate quest for profit with development that respects human dignity, environmental sustainability and decent work. Environmental sustainability is one of 17 fundamental enabling conditions for sustainable enterprises (ILO, 2007b). To that end, policies that enable SMEs to successfully navigate the shift to a greener economy and to seize the opportunities it offers will be critical. Cooperatives, business associations and partnerships along value chains can play an important role in supporting SMEs to grow and become sustainable. In addition to environmental regulation, research and development polices, as well as those on public procurement, need to be mindful of the needs and limitations of SMEs.

A recent study of five OECD countries found that SMEs welcome a standardized, rules-based approach to establishing environmental requirements (Mazur, 2012). Good practices for transforming SMEs include a sectoral approach to regulation, communication and enforcement; tailored regulatory instruments, avoiding activity-based regulation for low-risk installations; the use of economic benefits as a selling point; partnerships between regulatory/enforcement bodies and trade associations; and making green public procurement accessible to SMEs.

3.1.2.4 Environmental policies that address SME concerns

A growing number of countries explicitly address SMEs in their environmental policies: these include Malaysia, the Philippines, Sri Lanka, Singapore, many EU countries and the United States. Business development services can play an important role in helping SMEs cope with environmental challenges. Convinced that environmental sustainability will be a key factor for their competitiveness, the Brazilian small enterprise development service SEBRAE has recently made energy and resource efficiency, as well as access to green markets, one of its strategic priorities. Among its support measures, SEBRAE conducts attitude and practice surveys, documents good practices, provides guidance to credit lines for environmental investment and facilitates the link to buyers in value chains which put a premium on the social and environmental performance of their suppliers (see, for example, SEBRAE, 2012).

The key role of skills development in SMEs has also been highlighted, among other factors, in connection with the construction and agricultural sectors (see Chapter 2 above). In developing countries in particular, owners of and employees in small businesses tend to have insufficient business skills. Empirical analysis has proved that entrepreneurship training such as that provided in the ILO's "Know About Business" (KAB) and "Start Your Business" (SYB) programmes can be an effective way of addressing this deficit. Entrepreneurship training can also help small firms to identify green business options and turn environmental challenges into new business opportunities, an approach currently piloted with promising results in China and East Africa.

3.1.2.5 Promoting greening in SMEs and informal resource-based enterprises

Preventive policies, which preserve employment by reducing environmental impacts and risk, can also be applied to SMEs in natural resource sectors. An interesting example is the use of unemployment insurance coverage to ensure the reproduction of fish stocks in Brazil. The income replacement

---

Box 3.2: Social security and management of fish stocks in Brazil

Brazil provides an example of an initiative to extend social security to vulnerable workers in the informal economy. Artisanal fishers are entitled to unemployment insurance for the so-called closed period, during which fishing activity is prohibited to allow fish to reproduce. The length of the period is defined by the Brazilian Institute of Environment and Renewable Natural Resources (IBAMA) and varies across regions.

To be eligible for unemployment compensation, workers must demonstrate proof of registration as fishers at the National Institute of Social Security and pay contributions. They must also prove that they have no source of income other than that derived from fishing. The compensation paid is equivalent to a monthly minimum wage. In 2010, the Federal Government of Brazil paid Brazilian real (BRL) 34.2 million in unemployment insurance to 437,400 fishers. After 2003, the government loosened eligibility requirements, so that the number of fishers receiving benefits increased rapidly from less than BRL 100 million to more than BRL 1.2 billion in 2011.

Some aspects of the programme have been criticized. For instance, observers have noted that the existence of the insurance may attract new workers to the activity, which would increase fishing and run counter to the initial conservation intention of the programme. There may also be instances when access to the insurance is an incentive to disguise employment with larger fishing enterprises. While there may be scope for improvement in the design and implementation of the scheme, the Brazilian experience illustrates the way in which governments can use social security policies to protect natural resources while alleviating poverty among vulnerable groups.

Sources: Brazilian Presidency website: http://www.presidencia.gov.br; IBAMA website: http://www.ibama.gov.br/institucional/recursos-pesqueiros; McGrath (2012).

enables artisanal fishermen to respect the ban on fishing during the reproductive period of the fish. A major co-benefit has been the formalization of employment for over 400,000 fishermen (see box 3.2).

3.1.3 Dealing with job losses

Where job losses cannot be prevented, it is important that they are addressed proactively, as they are often concentrated in sectors and locations highly dependent on the industries affected and already under strain from decades of restructuring caused by globalization.

One of the keys to facilitating a just transition for workers will be early identification of affected industries, enterprises and workers, and the creation of placement and training services. The difficulty of adjustment for workers is often exacerbated by:

- The unexpectedness of the job loss

- Age, seniority, geographical and professional attachment to the occupation and lack of nearby alternatives

- A lack of awareness of policies and programmes that are available to help them retrain or switch to new jobs

3.1.3.1 Planning ahead for job loss due to green transformations

Since a green transformation can be anticipated to a certain extent, governments, business and labour can work together to identify potential adjustment pressures early, notably regarding skills deficiencies and upgrading, and develop strategies to ease the transition process. Moreover, public authorities could work closely with vulnerable sectors to inform workers, well ahead of any job separations or lay-offs, about the training opportunities and other active programmes that are available to them. At the same time, efforts will be needed to ensure that the education and training systems are responsive to the development of new technologies and economic growth sectors.

Prospective assessments such as those carried out with the help of the OECD model, or the forecasts for losses due to energy efficiency policies in China referred to above, are very valuable in detecting and preparing for job losses early. Economic modelling can be informed, complemented or even substituted for by direct feedback from the social partners who are directly involved in restructuring processes.

A widely cited example is the tripartite round tables of social dialogue set up in Spain in 2005. They were established to tackle compliance with the commitments under the Kyoto Protocol to reduce GHG emissions while checking the impacts on competitiveness, employment and social cohesion in the most severely affected sectors (ILO, 2010b).

Training, labour market and social security policies and programmes can play a significant role in helping employment adjustments by providing:

- Support to enterprises for retaining and/or retraining affected workers

- Matching of workers with new jobs

- Prompt identification of skill needs through surveys and other instruments

- Income support measures, such as unemployment benefits, to help limit the downside adjustment process for workers

- Information to workers on the range of active and passive labour market programmes available to them to minimize disruption

In situations where local and regional economies are heavily dependent on shrinking industries, efforts to diversify these economies may be needed to allow them to more readily absorb relocating workers, as illustrated by the experiences with restructuring in the forest industry in China and the fishing industry in Norway summarized below (see boxes 3.3 and 3.4). While a green transition is not unlike other structural changes, policies and programmes should nevertheless be tailored to address specific challenges and specific industries.

3.1.3.2 Addressing low occupational mobility

A factor which often complicates the transition for workers from resource-intensive or natural-resource-dependent sectors is their relatively low occupational mobility. This is partly due to a strong identification with their profession, for example among miners, steelworkers, fishers or loggers. It is also a consequence of a high share of workers with low skills or with skills and competences that are difficult to transfer and use in other sectors. As can be observed in table 3.2, for a range of industrialized countries (column 1) the total share of workers in the 15 carbon-intensive sectors which together account for more than 70 per cent of national GHG emissions is rather modest (column 3). However, in all countries except Australia, the proportion of workers with relatively low skill levels in the 15 top emitting

TABLE 3.2   Employment shares and skill levels in carbon-intensive sectors (percentages)

Country	Employment share in high carbon-intensive sectors (HCIS)[1] (% of total)		Share of low-skilled[2] workers in 15 most carbon-intensive sectors compared to low-carbon sectors (LCIS)	
	All HCIS	Top 15 HCIS industries	Top 15 HCIS industries	All LCIS
Australia	45	12	26	35
Canada[3]	48	23	–	–
European Union[4]	41	10	26	18
France	39	9	24	17
Germany	41	9	34	28
Japan	46	12	21	7
Republic of Korea	47	15	35	8
United Kingdom	38	7	15	10
United States	45	8	14	8

Source: ILO and IILS (2012a), p. 14.

[1] HCIS refers to all high carbon-intensive sectors (above the median) taken together. The top high carbon-intensive sectors include agriculture, mining and quarrying, and manufacturing transport.
[2] "Low-skilled" refers to education levels; therefore strict comparisons across countries should be made with caution. The employment shares of low-skilled workers are based on the total number of hours worked in the economy.
[3] Data are for 2005, except for Canada (2010) for the employment share (for the share of low-skilled it is also for 2005)
[4] Data for employment share in HCIS are for EU-15, whereas for the share of low-skilled workers they are for EU-20.

sectors (column 4) is higher than in those with below average emissions (column 5).

There are exceptions, though, which can facilitate transitions for workers and indeed entire sectors and countries. The existing knowledge and skills base in the offshore oil and gas sector in the United Kingdom, for example, is very relevant to the development of a domestic wind turbine manufacturing industry (CBI, 2012).

Skills in oil drilling could also be applied to geothermal development. Likewise, many of the skills employed in running fossil fuel power stations—including those of electrical engineers, electrical technicians, electricians and information technology specialists—can be adapted to operating renewable power plants (EC and ILO, 2011).

3.1.4 Integrated approaches for smooth and just transitions

3.1.4.1 What have we learned from previous industry restructurings?

Experiences with restructuring in different sectors and countries highlight some of the obstacles, but also contain encouraging lessons about policy mixes which are effective.

Poland's experience with restructuring its coalmining industry underlines the difficulty that workers may face in a broader move away from fossil fuels, as well as the need for a well-designed and fair transition strategy with adequate social programmes, retraining efforts and economic diversification of regions dependent on the coal industry. In Poland, unprofitable mines were closed down and coal production was slashed from 147 million tonnes in 1990 to 94 million tonnes in 2006. Employment fell even more dramatically, from 388,000 to 119,000 over the same period. The miners regarded the government's initial programmes to address the social consequences as unappealing, and funding was insufficient. Following elections, a new programme was formulated in 1998 with substantial trade union input. It strengthened social programmes and more than tripled funds in support of older miners made redundant, to about US$1.5 billion over five years. Out of the 103,000 workers who left coalmining between 1998 and 2002, 67,000 received financial assistance. Many of the miners had only vocational training specific to mining, and other sectors of the economy were also shedding labour. Thus, it took time for former miners to find work, but by 2003 as many as two-thirds of these workers were estimated to have found new jobs outside mining (Suwala, 2010).

It is worth noting that the Polish downsizing was prompted not by environmental factors but by global competition. Another consideration is the fact that moving away from the fossil fuel industry towards solar and other renewables promises substantial occupational health benefits. This is especially true with regard to coalmining. Although the work tends to pay well, it is one of the most hazardous industries for workers in terms of their long-term health and exposure to accidents (Summer and Layde, 2009).

The relocation of workers can be promoted by industry, by governments and in partnerships between the private and the public sector, as illustrated by the examples from the sugar industry in Brazil, the forestry industry in China, fishing in Norway and the steel industry in the United Kingdom. In all cases, diversification and the creation of alternative employment are keys to success.

UK Steel Enterprise, a non-profit-making subsidiary of industry giant Tata Steel, has helped workers to deal with the consequences for employees

Box 3.3: Restructuring in the forestry industry in China

Serious drought followed by a devastating flood in China in the late 1990s triggered national debates and reforms of environmental policies. Policy-makers and academics concluded that widespread and excessive cutting of forests and farming were the root causes. Measures taken by the government in response to these environmental challenges included a ban on logging on 73 million hectares of natural forests, equivalent to 69 per cent of the total natural forest area and to about 40 per cent of all forests in China (State Council of China, 2002). The ambitious ban on logging exacted very severe short- and medium-term social economic costs; in particular, almost 1 million state forest workers lost their jobs (Yang, 2001).

To integrate social concerns within the strategic environmental protection initiatives, measures were adopted to assist redundant state forest workers. According to the Chinese Ministry of Human Resources and Social Security (MOHRSS), design and implementation of the programme were based on consultations with tripartite committees at national and local levels, including the forest workers' trade union, with special communication channels being created for workers and farmers providing a telephone hotline, dedicated websites and microblogs.

Older workers were offered early retirement while younger ones could opt for education and training programmes through employment service centres and were supported in finding employment elsewhere. Redundant workers who voluntarily terminated their employment contracts and resettled themselves received a lump sum of up to three times their previous average annual wages. Up to the end of 2010, 680,000 redundant younger workers had received one-off payments, and 276,000 were re-employed or retired. Re-employed or subcontracted workers have been placed in afforestation, forest protection, rural infrastructure and public construction projects. Those who accepted lump-sum payments also received assistance to establish their own businesses (especially green businesses).

Approximately 100,000 redundant workers who were unable to find new jobs received unemployment support to cover minimum living expenses and medical care. A variety of social measures also targeted local farmers affected by the logging ban.

Source: MOHRSS (2011).

in the steel industry of a historical process of modernization and substitution of technology. UK Steel Enterprise was established in 1975 to support redundant steelworkers in their efforts to gain new employment. Seeking to improve the economies of regions most affected by changes in the steel industry, it provides tailored financial services for small business development, office rental facilities and local community development support. To date, it has helped to create more than 75,000 new jobs and supported more than 6,000 small businesses (Tata Steel Europe, 2014).

A challenge on an even larger scale was faced by the Chinese forestry industries and dependent communities when a logging ban was introduced over more than 40 per cent of the total forest area to stop flooding attributed to environmentally unsustainable practices in the forestry sector. Nearly 1 million workers lost their jobs almost overnight. A combination of income replacement, re-employment in the same sector, entrepreneurship training and assistance to create alternative employment and income opportunities targeted for different age groups of workers succeeded in a successful transition for 90 per cent of the workers affected (box 3.3).

In the Brazilian sugar industry a private–public partnership has been created to cope with the impact of mechanization forced by measures to reduce the impact of sugarcane harvesting on human health. Traditionally, the leaves of sugarcane are burnt prior to harvesting to facilitate manual cutting. This practice is being phased out, especially in the most important producer region, São Paulo State. The increasing mechanization of sugarcane cultivation and harvesting has reduced the number of direct jobs countrywide to about 304,000 in 2013, down from some 498,000 in 2007, although fluctuating volumes of production also play a role. Employment in sugarcane-based ethanol processing is not an option for the sugarcane workforce of mostly poorly educated migrant workers (in north and northeast Brazil, 55 per cent of sugarcane workers are illiterate or with low education, a much higher rate than in the south) (Soybean and Corn Advisor, 2011; MTE/RAIS, n.d.; Neves, Trombin and Consoli, 2010). The Brazilian Sugarcane Industry Association and other employers aim at retraining some 7,000 workers annually for a range of occupations, including as drivers, farm machine operators, electricians, tractor mechanics, bee-keepers and workers in reforestation (UNICA, 2009).

A very large transition challenge is faced by the fisheries sector, where 45 million jobs are at risk from overfishing. If addressed early and on a sufficient scale, a temporary transition programme for fishers could avert a longer-term decline in fish stocks and employment in the sector which may otherwise be difficult to reverse.

The case of the cod industry in the Norwegian Atlantic in the 1990s (see box 3.4) is a successful example of how practices such as temporary restrictions on fishing, and income replacement and retraining for fishers, have led to a recovery of stocks and new opportunities for displaced fishers.

Box 3.4: Norway's response to overfishing

As a result of the cod crisis of 1989–90, drastic cuts were made in the total allowable catch, and all the major fisheries were effectively closed down by 2005. As a result employment fell, driving fishers to find work elsewhere. Several remedies were offered, including debt relief. The Fishers' Guarantee Fund was established to provide temporary payments to fishers for loss of income, which dealt with the immediate effects of restructuring the fishing fleet. Resources were also provided for education and training to enable fishers to enter other areas of the labour market. Significantly, there has also been a concerted effort to expand the business sector by investing in the aquaculture industry and fish-processing market as well as non-fishing activity, so that retrained fishers have new employment opportunities.

So, while the short-term effects of the suspension of cod fishing were managed through various employment policies, longer-term challenges were met by rural and regional policies emphasizing education, training and investment. Norway was thus able to manage the resource crisis successfully, while stabilizing unemployment and migration rates. In fact, total catch sizes recovered quickly in the 1990s, while overall employment in the sector continued to gradually decline—to around 15,000 from a high of 115,000 in 1946. These two trends combined to raise the amount of catch per fisher to record levels. Ultimately, a total disruption and collapse of the fisheries was avoided, and the gradual adjustment that was required of the labour market was manageable.

Source: Hersoug (2006).

Programmes in Norway, and to a lesser extent in Canada and other countries, have been successful in reconciling environmental and social needs. They did, however, require investment to the tune of billions of dollars, in spite of the relatively small numbers of workers concerned. Providing this level of support to workers and communities during the transition period will be difficult in emerging and developing countries. The fishing communities in those countries tend to be significantly larger than in developed economies and many lack the institutional capacity to deliver a comprehensive suite of passive and active support measures.

An international agreement may therefore be necessary to restrict fishing by fleets from industrial countries in threatened fisheries and to help compensate small-scale fishers if temporary reductions in coastal catches of developing countries are also required. These programmes could be linked to payments for environmental services and coastal rehabilitation. They should also include measures to increase education and skill levels, diversify employment opportunities and promote SMEs in order to lift fishing communities out of poverty.

Investment in green industries can help overcome the economic problems faced by regions dependent on economic sectors in decline. For example, the Canadian province of Quebec used wind energy development to overcome severe economic problems in the Gaspé peninsula triggered by crises in the fisheries, forestry and mining sectors. Wind power tenders in 2003 and 2005 included a 60 per cent local content requirement (a policy meant to build local manufacturing and supply chains) within Quebec and a further requirement that 30 per cent of wind turbine spending take place in the Gaspésie itself. A centre for turbine maintenance (TechnoCentre Éolien) was set up, and the regional development programme "Action Concertée de Coopération Régionale de Développement" was launched in 2007 to promote economic innovation and employment in the province. Its efforts include the formation of a turbine manufacturing cluster. Gaspésie unemployment fell from 20 per cent in 2000 to 12.4 per cent in 2011 (OECD, 2012b). Similar economic transition and diversification efforts built around renewable energy development have been carried out in diverse places including parts of the US "rustbelt" (Pennsylvania, Ohio), in the province of Navarra (Spain), in Portugal's Norte and Alentejo regions, and at Germany's North Sea coast (IRENA, 2013, ch. 3).

3.1.5 Coherent policy responses can promote just transitions

On the whole, the restructuring from the transition to a more environmentally sustainable economy may be less pronounced than the changes wrought by globalization in recent decades. The dynamics and impacts will, however, vary from country to country and can be significant for resource-dependent regions and communities. Coherent policy responses and the involvement of ministries of labour and the social partners can help to limit the need for relocation and ensure just transitions where job losses are inevitable. Greening of resource-intensive enterprises, sectors and value chains, along with price signals through eco-taxes that favour employment, can significantly reduce job losses. Workplace cooperation and skills upgrading can be a powerful lever for reducing environmental impacts.

Anticipation and mapping of likely impacts are critical for timely and targeted measures. Customized policy packages combining income replacement and income security through social protection, economic diversification, enterprise development, reskilling and labour market placement have proved effective in facilitating smooth and just transitions. Enterprise development should pay particular attention to SMEs, which require appropriate regulation, information and support to master the transition and seize environmental market opportunities. Cooperatives and the social economy can also play a major role in a just transition and social inclusion.

3.2 Climate change adaptation and the world of work

3.2.1 Nature and scope of climate impacts

The impact of climate change on enterprises, workers and communities is highly location-specific and varies over time. In the short run, impacts are mostly caused by more erratic weather patterns and extreme weather events, such as heatwaves, storms, floods and droughts. These affect communities, enterprises and workers in exposed locations such as coastal areas and flood plains, including some of the world's largest cities. In developing countries, 14 per cent of the population and 21 per cent of urban dwellers live in low-elevation coastal zones that are exposed (Ten Brink et al., 2012). Extreme weather also affects exposed sectors, most importantly agriculture, but also tourism as well as drought-prone regions.

In the long run—and to an extent that depends very largely on whether measures are taken to sharply reduce GHG emissions over the next two decades—rising temperatures themselves will become a major factor of change. One of the consequences is that agricultural yields will fall in many areas. In some African countries, yields from rain-fed agriculture could be reduced by up to 50 per cent by 2020, and 75–250 million more people could be exposed to increased water stress (IPCC, 2007). Another consequence is that the areas suitable for certain crops will shift. In Chile, the agricultural belt is expected to be displaced to the south, shifting the demand for labour in agriculture and forestry between regions (ECLAC, 2009, 2010, p. 85, map VI.15). In Uganda, coffee growing will be restricted to the highest land, depriving the country of its main export and a source of employment (GRID-Arendal, 2002). In the short run, conditions would become more favourable for agriculture and other activities at high latitudes, but the overall economic impact is likely to be negative even in high-latitude countries (IPCC, 2007).

Rising temperatures are already leading to a melting of glaciers, including in the Arctic, where temperatures have risen twice as fast as the world average. The Greenland ice cap is losing 200 gigatonnes of water per year, enough to supply 1 billion people. The loss of glaciers and snow cover in the Andes and the Himalayas will put pressure on fresh water supplies and hydropower generation.

The melting of glaciers on land and the expansion of the oceans as they warm up has led to sea-level rises of about 20 centimetres during the twentieth century. This aggravates storm surges and leads to intrusion of salt water into fresh water reservoirs. A complete melting of Greenland ice—over several centuries—would release enough water to lift sea levels by more than 7 metres. Recent evidence from satellite measurement of sea levels does suggest that sea levels are actually rising twice as fast as predicted by Intergovernmental Panel on Climate Change (IPCC) models. By 2090 they may therefore rise by about 1 metre, rather than the 19–59 centimetre range forecast by IPCC in 2007 (Rahmsdorf, 2010).

Developing countries, and within them poorer segments of the population, are more exposed to climate change than richer countries and populations because of where they live and how they earn a living. They are also more vulnerable because they have the least adaptive capacity.

While it stands to reason that the disruption of economic activity, the loss of infrastructure and productive assets in enterprises, the relocation of enterprises and population, and reduced productivity will negatively affect employment and incomes, sometimes inducing or forcing migration, very little has been done to map and quantify these effects.

Environmental factors, in particular climate change, are already a strong driver for migration, both within and across borders. The UN High Commissioner for Refugees estimated that, in 2002, 24 million people around the world became refugees because of floods, famine and other environmental factors, exceeding the number of all other refugees including those displaced by armed conflicts (Warner et al., 2008).

The number of people who are forced to flee in the face of such disasters fluctuates markedly from year to year. In recent years, the total first declined from 36 million in 2008 to 17 million in 2009, then surged to 42 million in 2010, but then declined again to 15 million in 2011, only to rise to 32 million in 2012 and fall to 22 million in 2013. Except for 2008 (when 43 per cent of displacement was due to geophysical events), weather events have been the dominant reason for dislocations, and they accounted for 85 per cent of all displacements over the years 2008–13 (NRCIDMC, 2014). As climate change accelerates, the numbers are likely to climb sharply in future years. The Stern review notes that some estimates suggest that 150–200 million people may become permanently displaced by the middle of the century as a result of rising sea levels, more frequent floods and more intense droughts (Stern, 2007).

Migration is an important strategy for maintaining minimum income levels and has increased in recent years in response to greater variation in rainfall, particularly where there is no assistance to strengthen climate resilience *in situ* (Warner et al., 2012). For those with assets, in particular education and employable skills, migration is an opportunity; for those without, it effectively traps households at the margins of a decent existence. The combined effect—out-migration of those with skills and the staying behind of those without—has problematic implications for both environmental and social sustainability. The skills drain diminishes the capability of affected countries to embark on green policies and exacerbates economic and social inequality, which in turn may aggravate the environmental situation. Migration may thus relieve short-term pressures but could worsen impacts in the long run.

3.2.2 Assessment of employment and income impacts of climate change

Three examples of national assessments highlight the necessity and usefulness of analysing employment and income dimensions on a case-by-case basis, in order both to gauge climate impacts themselves and to design appropriate adaptation strategies.

In Namibia, a computable general equilibrium model was used to assess the economic and social impact of a variety of climate change scenarios (Reid et al., 2007). It concludes that even in the best-case scenario, 25 per cent of the population will have to find new livelihoods. The poorest households (subsistence farmers) are the most severely affected and will probably move to cities. As a consequence of the massive displacement of rural populations, incomes for unskilled labour in the cities could fall by 12–24 per cent, further exacerbating the situation of the poor.

The study of the employment impact of Cyclone Sidr, conducted with support from the ILO and Food and Agriculture Organization (FAO) (ILO, 2008), shows that methodologies to assess climate-related disasters must be sensitive to the characteristics of the sectors and types of enterprise affected if effective policy measures are to be designed (see box 3.5).

Box 3.5: The impact of Cyclone Sidr on enterprises in Bangladesh

When Cyclone Sidr hit Bangladesh in 2007 it had a direct impact on 567,000 people, corresponding to 14 per cent of all households in the 12 affected districts. Although 75 per cent were farm households, only 35 per cent had agriculture as their main source of income. Livelihoods and prospects for short-term recovery were therefore mainly affected by damage to income-generating assets in non-farm small businesses rather than harvest loss.

Damage to assets included the loss of fishing boats and gear, and of infrastructure, factory equipment and tools of self-employed workers. Private businesses included rice mills, sawmills, ice factories, potteries, blacksmiths and barber shops; equipment included tricycle vans, sewing machines and tools held in private homes. The damage affected about 30,500 establishments and 75,000 jobs. In addition, about 27,000 self-employed workers without fixed establishments lost their income-generating assets. The total value of lost assets was estimated at US$3.8 million, mostly in the manufacturing sector. Private businesses had to interrupt or reduce activity for more than two months because of the destruction of assets and the lack of electricity. The total loss of revenue in industrial and commercial establishments owing to reduced activity has been estimated at another US$47 million.

Enabling non-farm SMEs was the fastest way to restart economic activity, but required substantial access to new credit to replace lost assets. Interest rates surged in response, leading the government to impose a ceiling. This in turn resulted in a credit crunch. As the FAO/ILO assessment (ILO, 2008) revealed, high prior debt levels and an uncertain outlook made the SMEs high-risk borrowers. Credit guarantees of lower-interest government loans were therefore needed. Understanding the sectoral, employment and distributional income effects enabled the adoption of appropriate policies to accelerate recovery of income, notably in micro and small enterprises and industries.

Source: Government of Bangladesh (2008).

Adaptation measures can also have impacts on labour markets—sometimes inadvertent ones, as another example from Bangladesh shows (FAO, 2008). Dryland rice, the staple crop in north-eastern Bangladesh, is becoming unviable because of lower and erratic rainfall. Substituting mango—deep-rooted trees—for rice is technically feasible and economically viable, with a good market for mango. The labour market impact, however, would be significant, with a sharp contraction of demand for agricultural labour in districts where landless workers who earn their living as daily labourers in rice farming represent 41 per cent of the total workforce. Deprivation and out-migration would be likely consequences of the new cropping pattern.

Assessments of the employment and social impacts both of climate change itself and of adaptation to it should therefore be conducted systematically. Data should be collected about the labour market, households and enterprises. Enterprise data should encompass location, sector of activity, assets and number of employees. Employment data are needed broken down by sector, by gender, by formal or informal employment and by levels of skill. Household income and expenditure data should be collected by income quintile, differentiating between urban and rural households, between male- and female-headed households, and where appropriate by ethnic group, for example indigenous/non-indigenous households. In addition to income levels, the main sources of household income, assets and savings, as well as the affiliation of households with organizations, are important parameters for the design of adaptation strategies.

3.2.3 National initiatives on climate change adaptation

Significant climate change is already occurring and causing major damage to economies and labour markets. Even with drastic reductions of emissions today, global warming will continue for centuries because of the inertia of the climate system. Adaptation to climate change will therefore be essential to protect enterprises, workplaces and communities from negative impacts.

A range of estimates of the cost of adaptation have been made, based on different assumptions and scenarios. An early estimate by the UNFCCC in 2007 put global adaptation costs at US$49–171 billion per year by 2030, with US$27–66 billion needed in developing countries. A 2010 study by the World Bank arrived at a figure of US$75–100 billion per year in current US dollars for 2010–50 for developing countries alone. This is the same order of magnitude as development assistance by advanced economies to developing countries (World Bank, 2010). Other estimates are considerably higher (Parry et al., 2009).

Among the main policy responses by countries are National Adaptation Programmes of Action (NAPAs). All except one of the 48 least developed countries (LDCs) have prepared NAPAs, as have three other countries no longer on the LDC list (UNFCCC, 2014). Many more emerging and advanced economies, such as China and India, as well as Germany and the United Kingdom, have national adaptation programmes. Very few, however, explicitly address the employment dimensions of adaptation, which include:

- Rehabilitation of natural infrastructure and management of eco-systems such as water catchments, forests and coastal mangrove belts to reduce soil erosion, flooding or water scarcity

- Engineering options such as increased sea defences or storm-proof houses

- Risk management and reduction strategies such as early warning systems

- Access to social security benefits to buffer against shocks

- Development of financial instruments such as insurance schemes

- Capacity building of local institutions and communities, including the use of weather and climate data, adaptation of farming prac-tices, irrigation or water harvesting

Adaptation options are many, ranging from "software" measures such as training, capacity and institution building, and social assistance, to "hard-ware" measures such as infrastructure or reforestation. Well-designed national initiatives combine both types of measure. Public works pro-grammes or employment-intensive investment programmes, which have been used widely in the past in development programmes not necessar-ily related to climate change, can serve as a hub for a multifaceted inte-grated approach in adapting to climate change. When properly targeted and designed, they can help to reduce the vulnerability of the poor strata of the population by the provision of employment opportunities through a local resource-based approach. Through the right types of work and use of appropriate technologies, they can increase resilience to climate change and ensure a low-carbon or carbon-neutral approach to building more climate-resilient communities. These types of programme can have a mul-tiplier effect for employment, income security, climate-resilient asset crea-tion and access to fundamental services such as energy and water.

The restoration and protection of the natural resource base not only reduces climate risks but can improve agricultural productivity and income. Flood prevention measures such as diversion of floodwater and improved water management contribute to climate-proofing local infrastructure.

Large-scale public employment programmes such as the MGNREGA in India (see box 2.2 in Chapter 2), EPWP in South Africa (see box 2.7) and Productive Safety Net Programme (PSNP) in Ethiopia (see box 3.6) all make the link between employment, social protection and the restoration

Box 3.6: Ethiopia's Productive Safety Net Programme (PSNP)

Millions of people in rural Ethiopia are exposed to a potentially lethal interaction of drought and poverty. During the drought in 2003, 14 million people—one in every five Ethiopians—depended on food aid. Ethiopia's PSNP is a bold attempt to tackle the food security threats posed by an uncertain climate. Food insecurity is an integral element of poverty in Ethiopia. Traditionally, the response has been ad hoc food aid. The PSNP replaces this humanitarian model with an employment-based social transfer programme. Targeting people facing predictable food insecurity as a result of poverty rather than temporary shocks, it offers guaranteed employment for five days a month as a condition for transfers of food or cash equivalent to US$4 per month for each household member. Coverage has been extended from 5 million people in 2005 to 7.64 million participants as of 2012. At the same time, some 500,000 participants have graduated from the programme between 2008 and 2012. Unlike the food aid model, the PSNP is a multi-year arrangement financed by government and donors, shifting the mode of support away from sporadic emergency aid towards more predictable resource transfers and continuous investment. PSNP is enhancing community-level infrastructure and contributes to environmental transformation. Assessments also indicate that the programme has given families improved food security, increased asset creation and protection, provided better educational and health services, and improved agricultural productivity.

Sources: Gilligan, Hoddinott and Taffesse (2009); Sabates-Wheeler and Devereux (2010); WFP (2012).

and protection of natural resources. Although they may not all have been conceived as such at the design stage, these programmes illustrate the fundamental role public employment programmes play as part of social protection floors and how they can assist exposed populations to cope with the impacts of climate change and to adapt successfully.

Microinsurance and social finance can be valuable instruments to address climate along with other economic and social risks. Innovative finance schemes to strengthen the financial resilience of households affected by climate change have been developed in, among other places, Ghana and the Asia–Pacific region.

In the Philippines, microinsurance and finance as part of an integrated approach to climate risk attenuation has been tested by the ILO in a joint UN project on building climate-resilient farming communities through innovative risk transfer mechanisms. In the context of the so-called Climate Change Adaptation Project, a local financing and risk insurance model was designed for rice and maize farmers vulnerable to climate change in north-eastern Mindanao, in the southern Philippines. The project's model facilitated access to credit in support of crop production and alternative livelihoods as well as to savings facilities and to formal and informal insurance (covering crops, life and health), including the innovative "Weather Index-based Insurance" package. The project also facilitated access to productive services including training in farming technology (Farmer Fields School) and agricultural inputs. The technical training was complemented by entrepreneurship training, the promotion of financial literacy, and access to market information and business development services. As a result, these communities were able to continue with production in the face of climatic risks, diversify their sources of income, strengthen their asset base, and make more effective decisions on farming based on risk levels. At the end of the pilot in 2011, around 1,000 families had participated and had achieved an increase in net income. The project is now being scaled up with government resources and support from UNDP.[2]

While it is widely recognized that the approaches conducive to successful adaptation to climate change are similar to those appropriate for sustainable development more broadly, existing policies and strategies such as the NAPAs still pay little attention to the employment and income dimension. There continues to be a prevalence of technocratic and loosely coordinated measures. Integrated approaches built around social protection and employment promotion, such as those highlighted above, are proving to be effective. They can achieve both scale, as part of national schemes, and local relevance, being customized through local economic development approaches to account for the fact that the challenges and opportunities for adaptation to climate change are highly location-specific. A stronger participation of ministries of labour, employers' organizations and trade unions in the formulation of NAPAs and related programmes would provide valuable social and labour market information for the planning process, associate those directly concerned in implementation in the decision-making and thereby enhance the ownership and voice of businesses and workers, as well as synergies between public and private investments.

In addition to reactive adaptation efforts, there are also more proactive initiatives with an employment dimension. One recent example is found in a growing network of Climate Innovation Centres (CICs) (see table 3.3), which have been set up by the World Bank's infoDev Climate Technology Program

2   See http://www.ilo.org/asia/whatwedo/projects/WCMS_189793/lang--en/index.htm.

	Year launched	Companies/ ventures supported	Targets		
			Direct (direct + indirect) jobs after five years	Households with clean energy access	Project funds (US$ m)
Kenya	2012	70	930 (4,600)	9,100	15.2
South Africa	2013	n.a.	820 (2,469)	n.a.	21.2
Ethiopia	2014	40	700 (n.a.)	12,100	15.9
Caribbean	2014	85	370 (n.a.)	2,800	10.0
Vietnam	2014	66	700 (3,500)	7,400	17.9
Morocco	2014	60	n.a. (n.a.)	n.a.	13.9
Ghana	2014	Up to 194	632 (3,158)	n.a.	17.2
India	2014	70	970 (4,800)	17,600	16.0

TABLE 3.3   Climate Innovation Centres

Sources: infoDev (n.d.); infoDev (2010); World Bank (2014b).

with donor funding, with the intent to "help countries benefit from more pro-active participation in the ongoing global clean technology revolution, leading to economic gain and job creation, while reducing emissions". The expectation was that, in the first five years of their operation, these centres would create some 20,000 direct and indirect jobs, and possibly as many as 100,000 jobs after ten years.[3]

The first CIC opened in Kenya in September 2012, with the aim of providing incubation, capacity-building services and financing to Kenyan ventures developing innovative solutions in energy, water and agriculture. Over the next five years, it hopes to mitigate 1.5 million tonnes of CO_2 emissions, provide access to electricity for 1 million people and access to water for 440,000 people, and increase the agricultural efficiency of 22,000 farms (Global Green Growth Institute, 2014).

Ethiopia's CIC will collaborate closely with the government's Climate Resilient Green Economy strategy, and is aimed at accelerating "the use of emerging technologies in locally owned and developed solutions to climate

3   infoDev (n.d.) and other infoDev materials.

change". Funded by the World Bank and door agencies, it will provide financing as well as mentorship and advisory services to local climate innovators and entrepreneurs. The centre is expected to support up to 20 sustainable technology ventures in the first year of its existence, rising to more than 200 over the next decade (World Bank, 2013).

3.3 Adverse income distribution effects originating from energy poverty

The third category of challenges for labour markets and social inclusion arising from the transition to sustainable economies is of a different nature from the previous two; it concerns the impact that environmental policies to reduce GHG emissions and growing resource scarcity can have on income distribution and expenditure patterns of different social groups. Rising prices for energy—whether driven by scarcity and the pricing of GHG emissions, by levies to finance investments into renewable energy or by green energy subsidy reform—will have disproportionate impacts on poorer households. This is likely to exacerbate existing income inequalities within countries. This section examines the evidence on the relationship between household income and energy expenditure, and explores policy options for averting unintended regressive effects of policies.

3.3.1 Energy expenditure and income distribution

Environmental policies that raise prices for consumers can exacerbate energy and fuel poverty in both developed and developing countries. Energy-poor households are unable to meet their basic needs for energy even though they spend more than 10 per cent of their total income to this end. These households represent the extreme of a broader pattern: in general, poor households spend a higher proportion of their income on energy, despite the fact that they consume less and have far lower emission levels. These findings are confirmed by a number of recent studies for all continents. In much of Africa, Asia, Latin America and parts of Europe, the proportion of income spent on energy by poorer households is three times—and can be as much as 20 times—that of richer households.[4]

4 For more detail on the findings by country, see ILO and IILS (2012a), ch. 1.

Low-income households also tend to have lower income elasticity in terms of energy spending than those with higher incomes (Jamasb and Meier, 2010). This is further aggravated by the close link between energy prices and those of other essential goods and services, such as food and transport, on which the poor spend an even larger percentage of their income than on energy directly (see Chapter 1). The majority of poor households therefore have little budgetary flexibility, and an increase in prices or a change in energy policies can have a direct impact on them, forcing them to choose between energy payments and essential goods (Sustain Labour Foundation, 2008).

It is therefore necessary to keep these distributional impacts in mind when considering environmental transition policies such as the abolition of energy subsidies or the imposition of energy and carbon taxes. In addition to improving the access of the poorest to quality energy services, as discussed in Chapter 2, measures are needed to reduce the disproportionate burden on already poor households and the broader regressive income distribution effect.

3.3.2 Compensation for the impact of higher energy prices

Carbon-trading schemes and feed-in tariffs levied on electricity consumers tend to have stronger regressive effects than broader carbon taxes. Emissions trading concentrates on large point sources of emissions, notably power stations. Large industrial users are allocated emissions allowances and often exempted from financing feed-in tariffs, thereby shifting the burden to households and smaller enterprises.

Compensation for this effect through fiscal measures is not straightforward, because domestic use varies markedly between different groups and localities. While cash transfer programmes, for example, could in principle make up for such increases, such transfers are unlikely to fully compensate for the rise in energy prices. In the United Kingdom, even the most progressive use of revenues from carbon taxes to protect the poor would leave up to a third of low-income households losing out. This underlines the need to carefully design policies to address the effects of higher energy prices through a coherent set of policy measures, which can include transfer programmes embedded in national social protection floors and wider social security systems.

Gough et al. evoke possible alternatives considered for the United Kingdom (Gough et al., 2011). Figure 3.4 illustrates the pre-existing exposure

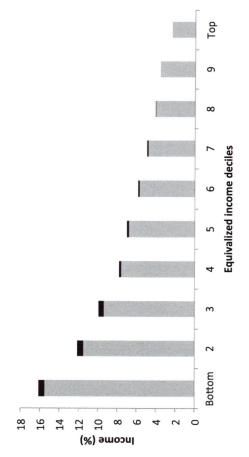

FIGURE 3.4   Energy expenditure with and without carbon pricing by house income group, United Kingdom, 2011

Source: Gough et al. (2011).

of households to energy prices and the expected impact of carbon pricing policies to reduce GHG emission levels—highest for the lowest income bracket.

To mitigate this effect, low-income price indices could be used to calibrate transfer payments. Differential energy pricing, at low cost for a basic consumption level and with steeply rising tariffs for additional use, would have a positive distributional effect. Such a block pricing approach is being used for water services in a number of cities such as Durban in South Africa and Dakar in Senegal,[5] but in the energy sector it signifies a radical departure from current pricing. The furthest-reaching proposal is a personal carbon budget, which would be complex to implement.

In the absence of readily applicable compensatory mechanisms, a radical expansion of eco-social investment in housing and transport infrastructure is widely seen as an essential complement. Such investments have been advocated by, among others, UNEP (UNEP, 2009) as a Green New Deal, i.e. an effective way to tackle the financial and economic crisis while advancing sustainable development goals.

5   See "Increasing price with volume", in UNEP and GRID-Arendal (2008).

Box 3.7: Brazil: Programa Minha Casa Minha Vida—PMCMV (My Home, My Life)

Initiated in response to a massive housing deficit, this social housing programme was launched in March 2009 with an initial budget of BRL 34 billion (US$18 billion) and planned to build 1 million homes for low-income families by the end of 2011. The second stage of the programme, which is integrated into the government's Growth Acceleration Programme (Programa de Aceleração do Crescimento), was announced in March 2010. With a budget of BRL 278 billion (US$153 billion) for 2011–14, it made a commitment to build a further 2 million homes. Families earning up to three times the minimum wage in cities with over 100,000 inhabitants will receive subsidies that set the monthly repayment rate to around BRL 10 per month. Families earning three to six times the minimum wage are guaranteed that their monthly mortgage payments will not surpass 20 per cent of their income.

Houses built under the programme have to meet a number of environmental requirements, including rainwater collection and the use of certified timber. Solar water heaters were made compulsory for houses in the southern half of Brazil in late 2010. The industry association ABRAVA estimated that some 1.1 million square metres of solar collector area would be added in 2011, surpassing the country's total installed area in 2008 of just 700,000 square metres. In 2009 the ILO (which advised the Brazilian Government to include solar collectors in the PMCMV programme) expected that some 500,000 houses would eventually be built with solar heating, and that homeowners could expect a 40 per cent reduction in electricity bills. The ILO also projected that nearly 18,000 additional jobs could be created in the solar installation industry. In 2010, the government-owned mortgage bank CAIXA financed approximately 43,300 housing units with solar water heating. CAIXA requires that solar installers working under PMCMV be accredited under the Qualisol quality label.

Sources: ECLAC and ILO (2010); Loudiyi (2010); Café (2009); Café (2010); Café (2011); Cardoso (2011). See also http://www.solarthermalworld.org.

Many countries are promoting energy efficiency in social housing and are expanding affordable public transport. The example of the social housing programme in Brazil, integrating solar water heaters (see box 3.7), illustrates the benefits. Electricity bills of beneficiary households decline 40 per cent, the national electricity grid saves expensive peak power supply and at least 18,000 jobs are added to the labour market. While solar heaters are a very effective and lasting way of addressing the root cause of the problem of energy poverty, it will take time for infrastructure development to relieve the burden on poor households.

Box 3.8: Cooperatives as providers of affordable clean energy

In some countries, cooperatives have traditionally played a major role in energy supply. In the United States, for example, 912 cooperatives account for 11 per cent of total electricity delivered, serve an estimated 42 million people in 47 states, and employ 70,000 people. In Argentina, the Sociedad Cooperativa Popular Limitada de Comodoro Rivadavia (SCPL) was founded in 1933 to provide energy at lower cost than the monopoly utility, when a group of entrepreneurs and socially active citizens bought the concession to distribute electricity. It later added power generation and built the grid which led to the development of the region. The cooperative has extended its activities to cover telephone services, the supply of drinking water, sanitation services and Internet access. Today, it has over 600 employees and owns the largest wind park in Argentina. Clean energy generation represents 17 per cent of its total energy production.

More recent examples are Greenpeace Energy (Germany), the largest energy cooperative in the country with 23,000 members and more than 110,000 clients (including 9,000 commercial customers). The cooperative was founded in 1999 to provide 100 per cent renewable energy at affordable prices by means of wind farms/turbines, photovoltaic plants and hydropower. With €101 million in sales, the cooperative has 70 employees. Overall in Germany, 47 per cent of the total installed renewable energy capacity of 73 GW in 2012 was owned by citizens and cooperatives (including 11 per cent by farmers). Just 12 per cent was owned by energy suppliers, 14 per cent by renewable energy project firms, another 14 per cent by industry, and 13 per cent by banks and investment funds (Leidreiter, 2014).

Inspired by the experience with rural electrification in the United States, the Rural Electrification Programme (REP) in Bangladesh was created in the late 1970s to make electricity available outside urban areas. As of August 2014, the REP included 72 rural energy cooperatives which generate and distribute electricity, employing about 16,000 people. The results of this electrification programme have been impressive: about 265,500 kilometres of distribution lines have been installed that now connect 52,525 villages to the electricity grid.

Sources: National Rural Electric Cooperative Association, "Co-op facts and figures", at http://www.nreca.coop/about-electric-cooperatives/co-op-facts-figures/; SCPL website, at http://www.scpl.coop; Greenpeace Energy eG (2014); Bangladesh Rural Electrification Board website, at http://www.reb.gov.bd/index.php/2-reb.

Another way of addressing the higher burden on the poor of energy expenditures, or simply of enabling them to access modern energy, is the formation of energy cooperatives. Cooperatives provide community ownership and control, while the priority of service provision keeps prices low. With the principle of sustainability for the community at their root, they also provide a voice to members and engage in dialogue on energy policy which facilitates community ownership, production and distribution of energy (see box 3.8).

In summary, higher energy and resource prices, caused by scarcity or policies to encourage energy efficiency and reductions of GHG emissions, will often have strong regressive impacts on income distribution, but this effect can be assessed and attenuated by compensating poorer households through transfers or adapted tariff structures. Transfers can be linked to existing social protection programmes and should be complemented by enhanced access to energy-efficient housing and transport for low-income groups.

4
Designing and implementing effective policies

Chapters 2 and 3 identified three areas of opportunities and three areas of challenges. There are significant opportunities to:

1. Create more jobs, particularly in green growth sectors, with net employment gains for the economy as a whole

2. Upgrade large numbers of existing jobs, making them more productive as well as more environmentally sustainable with massive benefits for poverty reduction

3. Promote social inclusion through access to clean, modern energy

The challenges result from:

1. The structural change associated with a transition to more sustainable production and consumption patterns

2. The already significant and growing damage to enterprises, jobs and livelihoods caused by climate change

3. The imperative to mitigate potential worsening of income distribution due to energy price increases

The examples of successful policy approaches have shown that coherent policies which integrate the three dimensions of sustainable development and which make use of the inseparable and complementary nature of productive employment, social protection, labour rights and social dialogue are the most effective in ensuring a smooth and just transition which seizes the opportunities and minimizes the social and economic costs associated with the challenges. More and more countries are embarking on a shift to environmentally sustainable economies and want to seize the potential to create decent work in the process.

This chapter presents a synthesis of major national and international initiatives. It also discusses opportunities for contributions by the ILO and provides a short overview of the current state of ILO practical support for decent work promotion in the transformation to greener economies, as a starting point for future work. The chapter then summarizes the policy lessons emerging from the previous chapters and outlines a conceptual framework for the contribution of the world of work to environmental sustainability.

4.1 Initiatives to promote environmental sustainability and decent work

4.1.1 National initiatives

Growing numbers of national governments are pursuing environmental sustainability, often with green economy and green growth initiatives, and increasingly with the support of employers' organizations and trade unions. Annex I, table A2, provides an overview of selected initiatives by countries at all levels of development from around the world. Many are recent, with a considerable number giving explicit consideration to green jobs policies or explicitly addressing jobs, skills, enterprise development, social protection and inclusion, and/or just transitions.

4.1.2 International initiatives

In the context of Rio+20, UN agencies and other international organizations have launched a range of initiatives to support growing worldwide interest in seizing the opportunities of a green economy. These initiatives aim at closing knowledge gaps by generating evidence, formulating concepts, methodologies and indicators, and identifying best practices. Several provide advisory services and capacity building, and engage stakeholders in policy dialogues. Efforts are also being made to step up finance for a greener economy. Only a few of these initiatives consider employment and social dimensions, however. The most relevant are summarized below.

4.1.2.1 Sharing knowledge

- UNEP has buttressed the findings of its landmark 2011 *Green Economy* report by posting online a series of success stories from around the world to encourage replication and scaling up. The experiences documented range from broad-based policies and practices to specific projects.[1]

- The UN Department of Economic and Social Affairs (UN-DESA) has developed a Green Economy Policy Map and Database. This searchable, online knowledge resource incorporates more than 300 examples of green economy policies, practices and initiatives and will become part of a new Sustainable Development Knowledge Platform.[2]

- The Green Growth Knowledge Platform[3] inaugurated in January 2012 brings together a global network of researchers and development experts to provide practitioners and policy-makers with better tools to implement sustainable development. The platform's founding members are the OECD, the World Bank, the Global Green Growth Institute (based in the Republic of Korea) and UNEP. The ILO has been invited to contribute specialized knowledge on employment, green jobs and social inclusion.

- The OECD has created a Forum on Green Skills, bringing together stakeholders in skills development for a low-carbon economy.[4]

- The G20 strategy on inclusive green growth adopted in May 2012 provides comprehensive guidance to member States, including on decent work, social protection and green jobs. An ILO/OECD issues paper on the implications for the labour market served as input. To assist implementation of the guidance, the G20 Development Working Group published a comprehensive toolkit jointly with the wider UN system, OECD and the African Development Bank (AfDB), including references to ILO employment assessment methodologies and the building of social protection floors (AfDB, OECD, UN and World Bank, 2012).

1   UNEP (2011c). See also http://www.unep.org/greeneconomy/SuccessStories/tabid/29863/Default.aspx.

2   See http://sustainabledevelopment.un.org/index.html.

3   See http://www.greengrowthknowledge.org/Pages/GGKPHome.aspx.

4   See http://www.oecd.org/employment/greeningjobsandskills.htm.

4.1.2.2 Advisory services

- A joint programme on "Supporting a Green Economy Transition in Developing Countries and LDCs: Building towards Rio+20 and Beyond" by UN-DESA, UNDP and UNEP promotes the green economy as a key element of "One UN" and UN Country Team programming. It supports about 15 countries to link sustainable development and poverty eradication.[5]

- UNEP's expanding Green Economy Initiative is currently providing policy advice, technical assistance and capacity building to 26 countries. Scoping studies and policy dialogues aim at determining key elements of a green economy strategy and roadmap. The ILO Green Jobs Programme has been complementing this policy design with assessments of the potential for green jobs where possible, including in China, Kenya, Mexico and South Africa.

- The UNDP/UNEP Poverty-Environment Initiative is assisting 22 countries to integrate pro-poor environmental sustainability issues into national development strategies, plans and budget processes. The initiative has supported work on protecting worker health in waste management.[6]

- UNDP also supports a number of countries in formulating green, low-emission, climate-resilient development strategies. Among the goals is the creation of new employment opportunities and green jobs.[7]

- The OECD's Climate Change, Employment and Local Development project aims to help national and local authorities promote good quality greener jobs in low-carbon activities. This includes efforts to measure the potential for green growth at regional/local level

5 See UN Sustainable Development Knowledge Platform: *Attachment A— Audit of current initiatives and key actors involved in Post-Rio+20 green economy work*. Available at: https://sustainabledevelopment.un.org/content/documents/1439AttachementA_Matrix%20summary%20of%20agency%20responses.pdf.

6 See http://www.unpei.org.

7 UNDP: *Green, low-emission and climate-resilient development strategies*. See http://www.undp.org/content/undp/en/home/ourwork/environmentandenergy/focus_areas/climate_strategies.html.

and explore ways to foster job creation and inclusive economic development.[8]

- The UN Secretary-General formulated a Global Action Agenda in April 2012 in support of Sustainable Energy for All, an initiative with three complementary objectives for 2030—achieving universal access to modern energy services; doubling the rate of improvement in energy efficiency; and doubling the share of renewable energy in the global energy mix.[9] Major new investments are to be mobilized, including through public–private partnerships.

- A 2012 report by the International Renewable Energy Agency (IRENA) finds that reaching the objective of sustainable energy for all could create almost 4 million direct jobs by 2030 in the off-grid electricity sector alone, and additional jobs relating to heating, cooling and cooking energy (IRENA, 2012). IRENA also calculates that direct and indirect global employment in renewable energy used for power, buildings, transport and industry could account for around 16.7 million jobs by 2030. This is up from a current estimated total of 6.5 million jobs (IRENA, 2013).

- The Director-General of UNIDO has launched a Green Industry initiative on resource-efficient low-carbon growth in developing countries.[10] UNIDO works with governments to support industrial institutions that in turn provide assistance to local enterprises and entrepreneurs, covering a broad range of issues including energy, resource-efficient and cleaner production, and management of chemicals, ozone-depleting substances and water. In collaboration with UNEP, UNIDO has set up a Green Industry Platform, a framework to bring together governmental, business and civil society leaders to secure concrete commitments and mobilize action in support of the Green Industry agenda.[11]

8   See http://www.oecd.org/employment/greeningjobsandskills.htm.

9   UN Sustainable Energy for All website at http://www.sustainableenergyforall. org. The Global Action Agenda is available at http://www.un.org/wcm/ webdav/site/sustainableenergyforall/shared/Documents/SEFA-Action%20 Agenda-Final.pdf.

10   UNIDO: *Green industry in focus*, UNIDO Green Industry Platform. See http:// www.unido.org/index.php?id=1001254.

11   UNIDO: Green Industry Platform website at http://www.greenindustryplatform. org.

- The Partnership for Action on Green Economy (PAGE), which brings together UNEP, the ILO, UNIDO, UNDP and the UN Institute for Training and Research (UNITAR), with the support of Finland, Norway, the Republic of Korea, Switzerland and a number of other donors, offers a comprehensive set of services to countries interested in promoting environmental sustainability with job creation and social inclusion. By early 2015, PAGE was offering customized advisory services for seven developing countries to help design, implement and finance policies and programmes, and to promote high-level policy dialogues as well as knowledge generation and sharing.

4.1.2.3 Finance

As adequate financing is critical for transforming the economy and the creation of green jobs, multilateral development banks are changing priorities and stepping up green economy finance:

- The World Bank's renewable energy portfolio has more than quadrupled from 2007 to 2012, rising to US$3.6 billion (or 44 per cent of the bank's total energy investments, up from 22 per cent) (World Bank, n.d.).

- In the transportation sector, the World Bank and the regional development banks announced at the Rio+20 Conference that they would make available US$175 billion over ten years for alternative, low-carbon transport (World Resources Institute, 2012).

- The AfDB is formulating a Green Growth Strategy focusing on providing sustainable infrastructure and efficient/sustainable use of natural assets, and on building resilience and adaptive capacity. The strategy is expected to guide the AfDB's operational engagement with its regional member countries and provide targeted assistance to countries committed to developing through green growth. Cape Verde, Kenya, Mozambique, Senegal and Sierra Leone have been identified for piloting national green growth support (AfDB, 2012).

- The Green Climate Fund set up under the UNFCCC[12] is to provide support to developing countries to help them limit or reduce their GHG emissions and adapt to the impacts of climate change. The fund is intended to play a key role in channelling new, additional,

12   See http://www.gcfund.org/about/the-fund.html.

adequate and predictable financial resources to developing countries, and should catalyse both public and private climate finance at the international and national levels. So far, the fund is nowhere near the envisaged level of US$100 billion per year.

• The UNDP/Global Environment Facility's Small Grants Programme provides funding for local-level investments into sustainable livelihoods. More than 15,000 community-level grants have been made around the world, some of which are directly targeting green jobs development.[13]

4.2 ILO support for environmentally sustainable development

Over recent years the ILO has significantly expanded its work to link environmentally sustainable development with decent work. Initial discussions led to the launch of the Green Jobs Initiative in 2007 with UNEP, IOE and ITUC. In response to strong demand from constituents, the Green Jobs Programme was established in 2008. In the light of the outcomes of the Rio+20 Conference, the programme's priorities were updated in November 2012 (ILO, 2012e) to focus on:

• **Capacity building for social dialogue**: strengthening training and outreach programmes to establish national frameworks and agree on measures that ensure a transition aiming at greater social inclusion and the creation of quality employment opportunities at sector and national level.

• **Employment assessments**: expanding ongoing technical assistance for the analysis of the employment impacts and implications for skills development of greening economies and enterprises at national and sector level.

• **Social protection floors**: identifying and promoting positive linkages between national social protection floors, economic development, poverty reduction and environmental protection.

13   See http://sgp.undp.org.

- **Research and knowledge management**: continuing to provide constituents with knowledge and information, tested tools and practical approaches on decent work creation in the transition to a green economy.

ILO headquarters, field offices, projects and the International Training Centre at Turin all participate in implementing the Green Jobs Programme. External partnerships, too, have been critical in achieving progress: these include collaborations with UNEP, IOE and ITUC under the Green Jobs Initiative; with other UN agencies such as UNIDO and UNITAR; and with a number of other agencies, including with the World Bank, OECD, UNEP and the Green Growth Institute around the Green Growth Knowledge Platform. The ILO is an active partner in the UN "delivering as one on climate change" and in PAGE.

4.2.1 Green Jobs Programme products

In order to effectively address the key links between decent work and the environment at national and international level, the programme offers global knowledge products, diagnostic and decision-making tools, capacity-building programmes, advice for practical approaches to green jobs promotion in existing and new enterprises, and support for just transitions for affected enterprises and workers.

A wide range of **specific products** have been generated in the process. These include:

- Global flagship reports on green jobs (UNEP, ILO, IOE and ITUC, 2008), skills for green jobs (ILO, 2011e; ECDVT, 2010)[14] and working towards sustainable development (ILO and IILS, 2012a), highlighting that green jobs need to be decent work in accordance with ILO standards.

- Documentation on the significant contribution made by social dialogue, from the enterprise to the international level (ILO, 2012f). The ILO Bureau for Workers' Activities has explored this in relation to a just transition (ILO, 2010c) and to international labour standards (ILO, 2012g), with a focus on tripartite consultation, the right to organize and collective bargaining.

14   For other products from the EC and ILO joint management agreement "Knowledge sharing in early identification of skill needs", see http://www.ilo.org/skills/projects/WCMS_140837/lang--en/index.htm.

- Customized capacity-building programmes for constituents developed and delivered in cooperation with other UN agencies, the IOE and ITUC, emphasizing tripartite consultation and social dialogue (see boxes 4.1 and 4.2).

- A practitioners' guide (ILO, 2011f) for quantitative ex-ante assessment of employment and income impacts of environmental policies and climate change, to inform responsive policies on employment promotion, equal opportunities for women, youth and disadvantaged groups, working conditions and social protection.

- Tested approaches and training products for green entrepreneurship and business development (Green Business Options, Green Value Chains, My.Coop) and greening of enterprises, including productivity improvement and clean production in Green Biz Asia and Sustaining Competitive and Responsible Enterprises (SCORE), translating into practice-relevant ILO instruments on youth employment, skills, equal opportunity, sustainable enterprises, working conditions, OSH and labour–management relations.

- Guidelines for labour in green construction and the built environment with a focus on working conditions, OSH and skills (ILO, 2012h).

- Policy briefs on gender and environmental sustainability, addressing gender equality in climate change (ILO, 2009c) and gender and green jobs. These briefs aim at a better integration of gender equality

Box 4.1: Promoting green enterprises: building the capacity of employers' organizations

A training manual is under development for employers' organizations in order to build their capacity to participate in national debates about greening the economy and to set up information and support services for member enterprises wishing to green their business practice and supply chains. The four modules of the manual are designed to improve the understanding and ability of employers' organizations to act in response to the implications of climate change and the opportunities in the green economy.

For example, the Mauritius Employers' Federation created a Green Enterprise Support Service in October 2012. The ILO Bureau for Employers' Activities and the International Training Centre at Turin have worked closely together on the manual and on training of trainers for interested organizations.

and women's empowerment in adaptation to climate change and in the promotion of green jobs.

- Research and policy briefs on safe and inclusive waste management and recycling, emphasizing the importance of access to adequate skills, OSH, equal opportunity and the abolition of child labour.

- Guidance on skills and enterprise development in renewable energy.

- An integrated approach to climate change adaptation favouring employment and incomes by linking public employment programmes, social insurance, enterprise development and local economic development. This brings to bear the ILO's value added on employment promotion, skills development, recommendations for SMEs and cooperatives, social protection (floors) and consultation.

Box 4.2: Sustainable development and decent work: a training manual for workers

The ILO Bureau for Workers' Activities, together with SUSTAINLABOUR and the International Training Centre at Turin, has created and implemented a distance learning training programme for trade unions in Latin America.[15] The course content and experience have subsequently been adapted for Africa. Interregional training courses continue to be provided in Turin, supported by an Internet-based platform. Overall, more than 100 trade union staff have participated, 45 per cent of them women.

The training materials available have been used by trade unions in many other capacity-building events. A recent example is the workshop on green and decent jobs for South African workers in November 2012, organized jointly by the Congress of South African Trade Unions and SUSTAINLABOUR with support from the EC and the European Trade Union Confederation. It covered topics such as opportunities for green job creation in South Africa, successful experiences already developed in the country, policy needs to ensure that the transition to a more sustainable development model benefits everyone, skills for green jobs, and the experience of trade unions and governments in other countries in relation to the creation of green and decent jobs.

4.2.2 Support for national constituents

Since 2008, a total of 37 countries have been assisted directly with capacity building and advisory services on green jobs, including 26 through technical cooperation projects (see figure 4.1). In addition, technical support has been provided to policy dialogues in a number of industrialized countries, including Canada, the United States, the EU and several of its member States. However, the increasing interest in green jobs and the demand for technical support outstrips current ILO capacity.

While the programme is relatively new, it has already contributed to a series of outcomes. Highlights of results to date include:

- **Bangladesh:** the government institutionalized and scaled up skills development for renewable energy with ILO support to increase the outreach of the ambitious SHS programme implemented by Grameen Shakti and other organizations (see box 2.5).

- **Brazil:** ILO participation in policy dialogues and advisory services was instrumental in including renewable energy in social housing and skills development for the new jobs created (see box 3.7), the mandatory inclusion of decent work provisions in contracts for forest concessions and the target for formalization of waste-pickers. Green jobs outcomes have also been included in the Decent Work Country Programme of Brazil and the Decent Work Agendas of the states of Bahia and Mato Grosso.

- **Chile:** the ILO provided technical assistance to an inter-ministerial task force established in 2010 charged with developing a policy for the inclusion of informal waste-pickers in the waste management sector. The task force conducted a study to analyse the current situation of waste-pickers in Chile. Building on the findings, the design and elaboration of a public policy proposal and action plan was adopted in 2013 by the Ministry of the Environment.

- **China and Kenya:** both countries are successfully testing training developed by the ILO on green business options for young entrepreneurs, and formulating policies and programmes for scaling up.

- **EU:** ILO participation in numerous consultations with the European Parliament, Council and Commission, as well as the preparation of two major studies for the EU by the IILS and the ILO Skills and Employability Department, has contributed to the inclusion of green jobs in the EU employment package (ILO and IILS, 2011).

Active Green Jobs support

FIGURE 4.1   Overview of Green Jobs Programme countries

- **Indonesia**: the Ministry of Tourism and Creative Economy revitalized 15 tourism destinations with the help of an ILO project on green jobs for youth, providing new opportunities for local communities. Drawing on this experience and extensive consultation, the ministry adopted a strategic plan for sustainable tourism and green jobs. In order to reduce and reverse GHG emissions from the loss and degradation of forests, labour-based approaches were introduced into Indonesia's forest rehabilitation programme.

- **Mexico**: as part of the development of a green economy strategy, the government conducted an assessment of the potential for the creation of green jobs and adopted a target. The goal is to double the number of green jobs during the period 2013–18 from the identified 1.8 million jobs related to the environment (representing about 5 per cent of the working population) in 2011.

- **The Philippines**: the country successfully tested an integrated approach to adaptation to climate change and local economic development, building on the contribution of an ILO project. The approach is being scaled up with government funding.

- **South Africa**: ILO participation in a national summit on the green economy, and follow-up assistance for employment assessment and the EPWP, contributed to the inclusion of green jobs targets in the national development strategy and its large-scale implementation.

- **Sri Lanka**: the country has initiated a programme to formalize and train waste management workers with ILO assistance (see box 2.3) and has included green jobs in its employment policy.

These examples show that great strides can be made when constituents are able to engage meaningfully in national consultative processes and strategies. An increasing number of countries are reorienting their development strategies, aiming for sustainable growth with social inclusion. The promotion of green jobs is part of a growing number of country priority outcomes, linked to employment policies, skills upgrading, employment-intensive investment, sustainable enterprises, sector strategies, and the eradication of child and forced labour.

The programme is in constant expansion and evolution. Updates on country-level activities and outcomes can be found on the Green Jobs website: http://www.ilo.org/global/topics/green-jobs/green-jobs/lang--en/index.htm.

4.3 Coherent policies for more and better jobs in a greener economy

A decisive turn away from the BAU policy scenario is urgently called for. A different set of coherent policies is needed if we want a fairer, greener and more sustainable future. Globally, the policy challenge is enormous. Most international policy institutions, among them the OECD, World Bank and UNEP, have made urgent calls for a change of direction (OECD, 2011; World Bank, 2012a, 2012f; UNEP 2011c). This has been accentuated further by the outcome of the UNCSD 2012 (Rio+20).

A greener economy requires sustainable production and consumption patterns; these will trigger modifications to practices in most enterprises and workplaces as well as structural change across the economy. The shift needs to create not only the incentives for enterprises to invest but also the capability for them to adopt new modes of production. A greener economy can be mutually reinforcing with good labour market and social development outcomes, but this does not happen automatically. It will hinge on the right policies and on institutions capable of implementing them.

The evidence suggests that gains and losses in terms of jobs, inclusion and equality are not happening by default, and nor can they be programmed with one-size-fits-all policy recipes. The shaping of the right mix of policies is very much country-specific. Countries and regions with large shares of resource-intensive and high-emitting industries face different challenges from those with a lighter legacy of unsustainable production patterns. The latter may have labour markets dominated by sectors exposed to climate change such as agriculture or tourism, affecting employment and incomes on a large scale.

4.3.1 Key policy areas

The main groups of policies which drive the transformation to environmental sustainability are:

- Macroeconomic policies, aimed at redirecting consumption and investment through price signals and incentives for enterprises, consumers and investors, including taxation, price guarantees, subsidies, finance and public investment.

- Sectoral policies for key economic sectors or important groups of enterprises, in particular SMEs. This includes most environmental regulation as well as mandates (such as the share of renewable energy in power supply, average energy consumption thresholds for car fleets, or biodiversity set-asides in agriculture and forestry). Most public investment in environmental sustainability is also aimed at key sectors, such as transport, land and water management.

- Social and labour policies, which ideally include a combination of social protection, employment, skills development and active labour market policies.

4.3.1.1 Macroeconomic policies

Macroeconomic policies are used to send price signals which reduce resource consumption and pollution, thereby providing incentives for investment and facilitating private-sector-led green jobs. They alleviate binding constraints identified for enterprises, thus creating an enabling environment. Such constraints often include lack of finance, inadequate infrastructure, inadequate and inappropriate skills, or prices which do not reflect scarcity and environmental damage. Since many of the investments have relatively long payback periods, a stable policy signal is essential.

Price signals are typically produced through taxation (a carbon tax or a "cap and trade" scheme whereby emissions limits are established and permits issued which can be sold). Incentives can also be created through guaranteed prices. Over 70 countries are applying "feed-in tariffs" which guarantee a price for electricity fed into the national grid from renewable sources. This temporary subsidy for cleaner power production is financed by electricity consumers. It has led to rapid deployment of renewable energy and dramatic progress in technology, increasing its competitiveness.

However, subsidies more often artificially reduce resource prices, stimulating resource consumption and waste. According to the World Bank, environmentally harmful subsidies amount to US$1.2 trillion per year (more than 1 per cent of world GDP): $0.5 trillion on fossil fuels, $0.3 trillion on water and $0.4 trillion on agriculture and fisheries (World Bank, 2012a). These subsidies constitute a strong disincentive for green investments and also tend to be socially regressive. The largest subsidies are received by the major consumers, which tend to be well-to-do households and enterprises.

Price signals are best transmitted through firm targets and strategies with time-lines. The EU, for example, has adopted the "20–20–20 targets" to reduce emissions, increase the share of renewables and improve energy efficiency by 2020 (EC, 2010). Brazil and Indonesia have both adopted unilateral emissions reductions targets below BAU. China has introduced goals for improvements in energy efficiency and the share of renewable energy in its five-year plan. The United Kingdom has adopted a climate change law to give such targets legal status. South Africa has included targets in its national development strategy. In the Republic of Korea, green growth has become the central tenet of the national development plan.

Other key challenges for fiscal policy and public expenditure management are sustainable financing of public investment in green infrastructure, and the inculcation of appropriate skills to meet the human resource needs of an eco-friendly economy. Without such a resource mobilization strategy, sectoral policies to promote green jobs are likely to become ineffective. Thus the current fiscal austerity programmes in the EU and other parts of the world may curtail green growth.

Green jobs have in fact been successfully "mainstreamed" through counter-cyclical policies. For example, during the global recession of 2008–09, over 70 countries accounting for well over 80 per cent of global GDP enacted fiscal stimulus packages. Public investment in green infrastructure became a common element in such packages (ILO and World Bank, 2012).

The effectiveness of green stimulus measures for employment creation has been confirmed recently by an ex-post study of the impact of the US American Recovery and Reinvestment Act (ARRA). Examining state-level data, Wilson (2012) finds that eight additional jobs were created or maintained for every $1 million of public investment. Total impact one year after the enactment of the law amounted to 2.1 million jobs or 1.6 per cent of total non-farm employment. These findings, based on econometric analysis, tally closely with ex-ante estimates derived from macroeconomic models such as input–output tables (e.g. Pollin et al. 2009; see Annex I, table A1).

Investment in public infrastructure can be a combination of fiscal (public) expenditure, social protection, employment and investment. Such strategies can be an important instrument with which to create a much-needed boost in employment and employability in rural as well as urban areas. Infrastructure is likely to be a key component of green economy and climate change adaptation strategies in most countries; many of the strategies and plans developed so far place significant emphasis on investment in infrastructure.

Monetary policies can also play a supportive role through the provision of affordable finance, credit guarantees and stable, competitive exchange rates.

As a package, such macro policies can have a strong "crowding in" effect on private investment, as demonstrated by investment in renewable energy globally and in energy-efficient buildings in Germany. Globally, investment in renewable power and fuels reached a record US$317 billion in 2011, a more than fivefold increase on the 2004 figure of US$60 billion. However, investments subsequently declined to US$251 billion in 2013—a consequence of cheaper solar panels and wind turbines on the one hand, but also a reflection of considerable policy uncertainty in Europe and North America on the other (Bloomberg New Energy Finance, 2014). In Germany, €21 billion of public investment (loans and grants) in energy-efficient buildings between 2001 and 2008 mobilized over €80 billion of private funding and permitted the renovation of 280,000 apartments and the creation of an estimated 221,000 jobs (Schneider, 2011).

4.3.1.2 Sectoral policies

Policies for key economic sectors and for industrial and enterprise development have proved important for a transition to greener economies, either as stand-alone policies or, more effectively, as a complement to macroeconomic and regulatory policies. As emphasized in the previous chapters and analysed in detail in recent reports by UNEP (UNEP, 2011c) and the ILO (ILO and IILS, 2012a), many environmental problems are sectoral and the search for solutions and adoption of policies accordingly starts at that level.

Many countries concentrate their efforts on the sectors that are most relevant in the national context. Examples include the "Grenelle de l'Environnement" (Environmental Round Table) in France, which focuses on energy-efficient buildings, transport and renewable energy, and China's new five-year economic development plan (adopted in May 2012), which has identified seven priority industries for growth and high-technology products. Alternative forms of energy, energy conservation and environmental protection, biotechnology, high-end equipment manufacturing, and clean-energy vehicles are expected to account for 15 per cent of China's GDP by 2020, up from 2 per cent today. South Africa's New Growth Path concentrates green investment on energy-efficient buildings, renewables and rehabilitation of natural resources.

Numerous countries have used industrial policy to support the shift to a greener economy. Examples include renewable energy in Brazil (initially ethanol, now biodiesel), China (all renewables), Denmark (wind) and Spain (wind and concentrated solar). Japan is prioritizing hybrid and electrical vehicles. The Republic of Korea is focusing on, among other areas, green information technology.

4.3.1.3 Social and labour policies

The transition to a greener economy entails both job creation and the transformation of many jobs and occupations, as well as displacement as workers change jobs, firms or economic sectors. In this context, labour market institutions and policies are critical for setting out the framework conditions for labour markets to adjust to the transformation required. One of the key areas of a policy package for the transition, therefore, is to enhance the capacity of the labour market to adapt to structural change, regardless of the source of this change. Employment, social protection, training and skills development, labour market policies, governance and cooperation between the social partners all affect the speed and form of adjustment.

4.3.1.4 Social protection

Social protection measures will be critical in the transition to a green economy. Strengthening social protection can:

- Provide the opportunity for poor people, including farmers, to adopt sustainable practices and improve productivity

- Afford income security and enable skills acquisition and mobility for workers who have to relocate to new jobs

- Remunerate environmental services rendered by poor groups and communities which engage in conservation activities and environmental protection

- Combine targeted access to employment opportunities with major investments in productive infrastructure, rehabilitation of natural resources and adaptation to climate change

People who are focused on daily survival and challenged by ill health, without access to social health protection benefits, are unlikely to give priority to conserving the quality of their environment and to engage in forest, soil and water conservation activities. A certain level of social health protection and income security is necessary to empower them to engage in such activities.

Some countries have explicitly incorporated environmental components into their social protection floor policies. The Brazilian "Bolsa Verde" programme (see box 2.6) includes a green grant designed to provide incentives to poor families living in natural reserve areas to engage in environmental conservation. Colombia and Mexico have implemented similar programmes. The Indian MGNREGA (see box 2.2) links a right to public waged employment with green infrastructure building and rural natural resource management to enhance the livelihood security of marginalized households in rural areas. Ethiopia's PSNP (see box 3.6) provides seasonal work in public employment programmes, remunerated in cash or food, in order to alleviate household vulnerability to food insecurity during the lean season.

These examples show that national social security systems, including social protection floors as laid out in ILO Recommendation No. 202, can make major contributions to enhancing people's resilience, strengthening their adaptive capacities and enabling them to seize new economic opportunities. The joint statement submitted by the AfDB, OECD, UN agencies (including the ILO) and the World Bank to the G20 Development Working Group argues: "Social protection instruments are a way to make green growth more inclusive and socially acceptable" (AfDB et al., 2012). Social protection floors need to be defined in each specific country context, typically building on existing (though often inadequate) social protection schemes.

4.3.1.5 Vocational training and skills development

Training and skills development policies will require considerable attention. Skills are fundamental to adjusting worker competencies to evolving demand for jobseekers, changing competencies in occupations and the need to relocate. The ILO global study on skills for green jobs (ILO, 2011e) has shown that shortages of qualified workers are already hampering the shift to a greener economy in most countries and sectors, because demand has been underestimated or skills systems are not linked to macroeconomic and sectoral policies for greening. This is a critical point, because without skilled workers and competent enterprises the shift to a greener economy will be neither technically feasible nor economically viable.

The extent of the transition in skills and occupations depends on several factors, including country-specific industrial structure and stage of development. Nevertheless, some important general lessons have emerged (ILO, 2011g):

- **Place emphasis on skills and education policies to facilitate job transition and improve employability**: a greener economy will see the emergence of some new occupations, but it will mostly require new competencies in existing jobs and bring shifts in demand for occupations. This means that greater emphasis needs to be placed on skills upgrading through workplace training, as well as on preparing new generations of workers. There is ample evidence from around the world that it is both possible and necessary to anticipate future skill needs and make adjustments in education and training systems. Australia, Europe and the United States are leading in mapping new skills requirements, including those for safe and healthy work practices.

- **Link training systems more directly to evolving demand:** in order to respond quickly and appropriately to the emerging demand in green growth sectors, training initiatives should target the environmental goods and services sector, where expansion will create new demands for a variety of skill profiles. Tripartite skills councils, as in France and the Republic of Korea, are a good way of making training systems more responsive. Other examples include the Green Skills Agreement in Australia, the UK Alliance of Sector Skills Councils (SSCs), the mobilization plan for green jobs in France and the Fund for Energy Savings bringing together utilities, trade unions and enterprises in Mexico.

- **Ensure equal access:** experience shows that those who have the required skills are also the ones who find jobs. Skills can therefore be an important stepping stone for giving young women and men and other disadvantaged groups access to the job and income generation opportunities created in a green economy.

- **Encourage acquisition of generic and science, technology, engineering and mathematics (STEM) skills:** core skills are increasingly important, and STEM skills especially so: these will be needed for new research and development to achieve breakthroughs for greening economies. They will also enhance labour force mobility generally.

- **Promote "portable skills":** this is best done through qualifications based on competency profiles for green jobs which are recognized sector-wide. A good example is the tripartite creation of certification of green plumbers in Australia (ILO, 2011e).

- **Address the significant reskilling needs for greening as well as relocation:** this is particularly important for workers in resource-intensive sectors such as mining, power generation, manufacturing and agriculture.

- **Integrate skills into policies for climate change adaptation**: the skills required for successful adaptation to climate change will depend on the sectors concerned and the adaptation strategies chosen. Skills development has so far rarely been recognized as an adaptive response in national adaptation plans of action. If it was, it could for example be delivered as part of public employment programmes providing retraining and skills upgrading for workers to become employable in transformed, more environmentally friendly jobs.

4.3.1.6 Sustainable enterprise development

The social, economic and environmental dimensions of sustainable development come together inseparably in enterprises and workplaces. Enterprises not only employ the majority of the global workforce and act as a main driver of employment creation and wealth generation, but they are also vital for environmental sustainability. Enterprises will have to be able to produce a wider range of green goods and services and to adopt clean production methods. Successful policies to facilitate this shift include:

- An enabling environment for sustainable enterprises generally, but specifically regulatory and fiscal measures which promote demand for green products and services and drive green investments

- Special consideration to help SMEs comply with environmental regulation and to seize green business opportunities, along with a sectoral approach to regulation, communication and enforcement, with tailored regulatory instruments and partnering between regulatory/enforcement bodies and trade associations

- Uptake of green business opportunities, achieved by business development services including green entrepreneurship training, access to information, technology, credit and markets, and through making green public procurement accessible to SMEs

- Greening of all existing enterprises, with a strong role for skills upgrading and management–worker cooperation at sectoral and enterprise levels, which in many cases can build on institutions and practices already existing to promote OSH

- Value chain development by enterprises themselves or in partnership with government institutions, which can be effective in identifying opportunities for reducing environmental impact and expanding green business opportunities

- Development of resilience to climate change on the part of businesses to avoid disruption of economic activity and loss of jobs and income; to this end, national policies and plans for adaptation should work closely with business associations to climate-proof infrastructure and promote disaster-preparedness information, skills development and insurance, in particular for SMEs

- A pivotal role for cooperatives in enhancing climate resilience but also in seizing green business opportunities and developing value chains

4.3.1.7 Occupational safety and health (OSH)

As the green economy develops it is essential that the safety and health of workers are integrated into policies for the transition to green jobs. The current focus on a low-carbon economy should integrate environmental aspects with OSH and public health, while at the same time taking into consideration the well-being of surrounding communities.

Integrating the OSH dimension implies evaluating the hazards and risks to workers in all green jobs, processes and products through the implementation of risk assessment and management measures. For jobs to be truly green, safety and health must be integrated into design, procurement, operations, maintenance, sourcing, use, reuse and recycling policies and decision-making as part of national OSH policies.

Government policy, labour inspection, social dialogue and collective bargaining on OSH issues, as well as corporate governance, can play key roles in prevention, reporting and enforcement to ensure that green jobs are safe and traditional jobs become safer. ILO standards on safety and health promote universal principles which are pertinent to any type of economic system or workplace, but some are also directly relevant to the protection of the environment. This is particularly true for the Chemicals Convention, 1990 (No. 170), and the Prevention of Major Industrial Accidents Convention, 1993 (No. 174).

Effective labour inspections are critical for the implementation of, and adherence to, labour legislation. Labour inspectors examine how labour standards are applied in the workplace and advise how the application of national law in matters including working time, wages, OSH and child labour can be improved. The importance of labour inspections has been recognized in two labour inspection Conventions. To date, more than 130 countries have ratified the Labour Inspection Convention, 1947 (No. 81), and more than 40 have ratified the Labour Inspection (Agriculture) Convention, 1969 (No. 129), though there are challenges in countries where inspection systems are underfunded and understaffed.[16]

4.3.1.8 Labour market policies

The existing suite of active and passive labour market policies can play a significant role in helping to realize the opportunities for more and better jobs as well as fostering social inclusion. Active labour market policies encompass a broad set of policies with different aims: supporting labour demand by maintaining jobs or directly creating new jobs, and maintaining links to the labour market, in particular through jobsearch assistance and access to training.

In many instances of adjustment this may simply require augmenting the existing suite of active labour market programmes such as jobsearch assistance, job counselling, training and improved labour market information. This will reinforce the adaptive capacity of the labour market, and not just in the context of a green economy. In developing countries, however, as discussed above, programmes of this nature are still limited, and efforts to develop strong labour market institutions are thus needed.

Some labour market policies, such as jobsearch assistance, do not need deep reform but can also play a role if they are tooled to assist the transition. Jobsearch assistance is a relatively effective and low-cost tool to reduce unemployment and the risk of skills degradation. Awareness of the opportunities in a greener economy and skills requirements for green jobs among workers and employers, as well as employment services, can be raised through institutions such as France's National Observatory for Green Employment and Occupations, but typically also requires capacity building in employment services.

In developing countries, public employment programmes and employment guarantees play an important role in sustaining labour demand. These programmes can be "greened" by entering directly into environmental services or by producing greener infrastructure. Another role for such

16   ILO: "International labour standards on labour inspection", at http://ilo. org/global/standards/subjects-covered-by-international-labour-standards/labour-inspection/lang--en/index.htm.

programmes is to transfer the skills needed for workers to be employable in transformed, more environmentally friendly jobs.

In some instances, bolstering the existing range of programmes may be insufficient and a degree of tailoring will be required—particularly relevant given the fact that challenges are often sector-specific. Examples include the Belgian public employment service, which has developed a "sustainable building" competency centre in East Flanders. In addition to practical skills training, such as learning how to install eco-efficient heating, the centre matches workers and engineers with green building skills to demand in the construction sector (Intelligent Energy Europe, 2012). And in the Brussels region of Belgium, the construction sector, trade unions and public authorities joined forces to establish the Professional Reference Centre for Construction (Centre de Référence Professionnel de la Construction) to address skills shortages in eco-construction, renovation and retrofitting, by bringing together employment and training services, educational institutions and the construction sector.[17] Similarly, in Morocco the public employment service ANAPEC is managing the recruitment process for major green construction works.[18]

4.3.2 Policy coherence: objectives and examples

Four policy objectives are key to achieving win–win outcomes:

1. Shifting the tax burden away from labour and towards resource use and pollution

2. Encouraging investment in a greener economy

3. Providing targeted support to enterprises, notably SMEs

4. Ensuring just transitions for workers negatively affected by restructuring, for communities exposed to climate change and for population groups disadvantaged by green policies

The most successful examples are characterized by the purposeful matching of economic, environmental and social policies.

Among macroeconomic policies, eco-taxes have emerged as an instrument of choice because they integrate both dimensions in a single tool. Eco-taxes can generate a double dividend of improved environmental

17   Centre de Référence Professionnel de la Construction: "Nature de l'activité du CDR construction", http://www.cdr-brc.be/fr/default.asp.

18   See http://www.anapec.org.

sustainability and net gains in employment (compared with BAU) when revenue generated to increase the price of resource consumption is used to stimulate employment by investing in human resources and reducing the price of labour.[19] Eco-taxes are a powerful policy lever, and will work best if complemented by other policies such as skills and enterprise development. Harmonized approaches across different policy fields in key economic sectors include:

- **Agriculture:** resource conservation and low-carbon agriculture, enabling small-scale producers to adopt more productive and sustainable production methods through technical and entrepreneurial skills, supportive social protection, targeted investment in infrastructure, organization and finance (see examples from Ethiopia (box 3.6), India (box 2.2), and the Philippines (Chapter 3)).

- **Forestry:** arresting deforestation, rehabilitating degraded forests and extending sustainable forest management through support for sustainable forest enterprises with high skill levels and good working conditions, value-chain development and payment for environmental services to local communities which can be linked to social protection floors (see examples from Brazil and South Africa in Chapter 2).

- **Fisheries:** reducing overfishing, allowing depleted stocks to recover and promoting sustainable levels of catch by providing income replacement during unemployment; access to employable skills outside fishing and promotion of alternative income opportunities (see examples from Brazil (box 3.2) and Norway (box 3.4)).

- **Energy:** improved energy efficiency through regulation, price signals and access to finance, supported by skills upgrading and labour management cooperation; deployment of renewable energy with access for those currently without modern energy through targeted SME development, cooperatives and social housing (see example from Brazil (box 3.7).

- **Resource-intensive industries:** stimulating greening of these industries to substantially reduce pollution, energy and resource consumption through regulation and incentives, coupled with

---

19   For a detailed discussion of empirical and modelling evidence, see ILO and IILS (2012a), ch. 10.

information, access to finance and management-worker cooperation at sector and enterprise levels (see examples from Japan, the
Republic of Korea (both Chapter 3) and 3M (box 3.1)).

- **Waste management and recycling:** reducing hazards from waste
and expanding recovery of valuable material by increasing recycling and upgrading informal waste management through organization of informal recycling workers, service contracts, technical
and business skills development (see examples from Brazil and Sri
Lanka (box 2.3)).

- **Buildings:** tapping the largest potential for energy efficiency gains
by adopting high building standards for new construction, and
stimulating renovation of existing building infrastructure by regulation, information, public investment and access to affordable
finance for clients and skills upgrading, certification of competences and improvement in working conditions in the building sector (for examples, see Chapter 2).

- **Transport:** shifting to energy-efficient vehicles and modes of transport, in particular public transport, through fiscal policies, regulation and incentives for consumers in combination with technology
development, skills upgrading and public investment in infrastructure (see examples from China, Japan and the Republic of Korea in
Chapter 2).

Examples of countries which have successfully adopted an integrated
sector focus include:

- **China,** which has supported environmental and labour market
goals with a successful green stimulus package during the economic
crisis, creating 5.3 million jobs in the green economy between 2009
and 2012. Targets for energy efficiency and renewables in national
development plans are matched by targets for green job creation.
The latter are supported through development of vocational and
entrepreneurship skills as well as assistance to green business
start-ups.

- **Austria's** "Klima-aktiv" (Active for the Climate) policy, launched
in 2004, which has been very successful in giving SMEs access to
opportunities in a greener economy, particularly in green construction and renewable energy. Environment policies are coordinated

with those for the labour market, in particular workforce training, quality standards for new products and services, information and communication campaigns, and advice and support to businesses and networking.

To complement national and sector-focused policies, local economic development strategies can be pursued in realizing a growth path with low environmental impact and high employment and income benefits. Measures can be adopted and integrated to respond to local needs, constraints and opportunities in the green economy through inclusive and participatory planning and implementation. Local employment and value added can be multiplied when adopting appropriate technology and relying on local resources to improve the natural resource base and to climate-proof private and public infrastructure, especially when using local SME contractors.

4.3.3 Achieving policy coherence: assessments, institutions and social dialogue

Coordinated implementation across policy areas is particularly important. Unlike recent major structural transformations brought about by globalization or by the ICT revolution, the transformation to a more sustainable economy is likely to be largely policy-led.

4.3.3.1 Assessing social impacts for more effective strategies

One of the key ingredients for successful policy-making has been ex-ante assessment of the expected impact of specific greening policy measures. This enables decision-makers to clarify the link between environmental issues and policies on the one hand, and effects on social groups and social objectives on the other—including employment creation and the generation and distribution of income. Ideally, such analysis would be used to prioritize policy options. These changes can be anticipated better than for adjustments arising from other causes, so that the transition can be managed more smoothly and possibly more fairly.

As we have seen in this book and other earlier reviews (UNEP, 2011c; UNEP, ILO, IOE and ITUC, 2008; ILO and IISS, 2012), the environmental challenges, as well as the options for addressing them, differ widely between countries and between economic sectors. Assessments can do justice to this diversity by taking account of specific national, sectoral or local conditions.

A range of methods are available and have been applied to understand the interlinkages between the environmental, economic and social dimensions of the transformation to sustainable production and consumption patterns. No single method can provide all the answers; each has its strengths and weaknesses in terms of data needs, level of detail captured, ability to take account of interlinkages within the economy, and time-horizon. There are often trade-offs between these parameters: for example, a method for economy-wide analysis over a longer time-horizon typically has high data requirements and limited resolution.

These constraints and trade-offs notwithstanding, several assessment methods have been helpful for informing policy (see examples in Annex I, table A1). Useful methods include sector studies, input/output (I/O) analysis, static or dynamic social accounting matrices (SAM/DySAM) and computable general equilibrium models, as well as a variety of complex dynamic models which use systems analysis and sometimes combine physical and economic variables.

Some countries have conducted assessments of environment-related employment for many years and monitor it periodically. In Germany, assessments started in 1994 and analyses of employment effects of environmental policies have been conducted for over a decade.[20] In recent years, a growing number of countries have begun to collect such data.

4.3.2 The contribution of social dialogue

Social dialogue aims to promote consensus building among the major stakeholders. Effective dialogue can help to resolve crucial socio-economic issues and improve economic performance. Given that the transition towards a greener economy will entail profound changes in production processes and technologies as well as reallocations of jobs, close cooperation between government and the social partners will be central to the success of this transformation. The need for participation in governance was already recognized in Agenda 21 and has been emphasized even more in the Rio+20 outcome document.

Numerous examples in this book[21] highlight the critical role played by social dialogue, at all levels from international, through national and sectoral to local and enterprise, in:

20   See German Ministry of Environment website at http://www.germany.info/
      contentblob/3146650/Daten/1312974/BMU_GrosEmploymentRE2010_DD.pdf.
21   See also ILO (2013c).

- Informing policy
- Promoting policy coherence
- Launching initiatives for greening the economy and enterprises
- Forming partnerships for the implementation of policies
- Promoting job quality and decent work in green sectors and occupation
- Sensitizing, advising and assisting the members of employers' organizations and trade unions

Social dialogue informs policy-making by contributing essential information to assessments. The perspectives of the social partners ensure that social outcomes are taken into account and that social and labour market policies can complement environmental and economic measures. Existing forums such as the councils for social and economic development in many countries, or new ones such as the "Grenelle de l'Environnement" in France or the tripartite round tables for the implementation of the Kyoto Protocol in Spain, have been instrumental in forging agreements on large, integrated policy packages. An outstanding example of an initiative driven by the social partners is the German programme for energy efficiency in buildings (see Chapter 2). Examples for sectoral and enterprise-level initiatives from Japan, the Republic of Korea, the United States and others were reviewed in Chapters 2 and 3. In South Africa, the "green economy accord" has been concluded to formalize the partnership between relevant line ministries and the social partners for the implementation of this component of the national development plan.

Employers' organizations and trade unions have sensitized and provided advice to their memberships in many countries. In Latin America, for example, over 2,500 trade union members have completed a distance learning course on sustainable development. There has also been innovation in collective bargaining: for example, collective agreements in Belgium include an incentive to buy sustainably produced products.

4.4 Towards a policy framework for sustainable development with decent and green jobs

The review of experiences throughout this book, and in particular the rapidly growing number of national and international initiatives discussed, clearly shows that the search for a fairer, more inclusive and environmentally sustainable development model has gained momentum in many countries. This search is spurred on by the realization that environmental sustainability is not optional, but a necessity, including for labour markets, sustainable enterprises and poverty reduction.

Achieving environmental sustainability requires profound and far-reaching changes in production and consumption patterns. Efforts towards this goal are already having major impacts in workplaces and enterprises, in labour markets and in communities. The environment is clearly a social and labour issue. Decent work can only play its role as a driving force for sustainable development if this linkage to the environment is acknowledged and factored into policies and practices.

The Rio+20 Conference underlined the importance of overcoming thinking, policy-making and actions based on a concept of sustainable development with three separate pillars. The challenge for the future is to recognize and act on the linkages between the economic, social and environmental dimensions. This book has shown that environmental sustainability cannot be achieved without the active engagement of the actors in the world of work. By contrast, where the links are recognized, the social and environmental dimensions can become mutually supportive, and even challenges such as the need to adapt to climate change can be turned into opportunities.

Macroeconomic and environmental policies, coupled with investment in a skilled workforce and opportunities in enterprises, can create a powerful dynamic for sustainable development. Social housing policies stimulating local SMEs in a greening construction sector, or promoting renewable energy with skills training and entrepreneurship promotion for women and youth, promote social inclusion and create jobs while avoiding an unsustainable environmental footprint. Linking labour inspection and the prevention of major industrial accidents to environmental regulations in forestry and mining and to the development of local and global value chains enhances the development contribution of extractive sectors while containing their environmental impact.

Table 4.1   The contribution of the world of work to environmentally sustainable development

Contribution	Economic	Social	Environmental
Goals	1. **Create opportunities** for productive employment in environmentally sustainable sectors and enterprises 2. **Reduce the economic cost of transition** due to the labour market	1. **Provide access to quality jobs and income opportunities** for unemployed, underemployed and working poor 2. **Promote a just transition** with a fair sharing of cost and opportunity	1. **Adopt green products and practices in enterprises and at workplaces** (bring about environmental sustainability of key sectors and economies as a whole) 2. **Enhance resilience to climate change** of enterprises, workplaces and communities
Relevant measures and policies: • International labour standards (ILS) providing guidance on substance	• Employment creation (Employment Policy Convention, 1964 (No. 122)) • Labour force development (Human Resources Development Convention, 1975 (No. 142)) • Enterprise development (Job Creation in Small and Medium-sized Enterprises Recommendation, 1998 (No. 189); Promotion of Cooperatives Recommendation, 2002 (No. 193); Multinational Enterprise Declaration)	• Quality job opportunities (ILS on working conditions, social protection, social protection, representation) • Equitable access (ILS on non-discrimination, skills, social security) • Just transition for those who lose jobs or livelihoods (ILS on dismissal, social protection, reinsertion, migration)	• Adopt green products, services, processes and practices (resource and energy efficient; minimum pollution) • Social protection, skills development, economic diversification (ILS on SMEs, on OSH, human resources development and social protection, in particular the Social Protection Floor Recommendation, 2012 (No. 202))
Relevant measures and policies: • ILS providing guidance on governance	• Consultation and participation (Tripartite Consultation (International Labour Standards) Convention, 1976 (No. 144); Indigenous and Tribal Peoples Convention, 1989 (No. 169))	• Participation in enterprises (Freedom of Association and Protection of the Right to Organise Convention, 1948 (No. 87); Right to Organise and Collective Bargaining Convention, 1949 (No. 98) and communities (Conventions Nos 144 and 169))	• Participation in enterprises (Conventions Nos 87 and 98) • Workplace cooperation (Benzene Convention, 1971 (No. 136))

The overarching challenge for ILO constituents is to leverage the process of structural change towards sustainable production and consumption patterns for the large-scale creation of quality employment opportunities, the extension of adequate social protection, the advancement of social inclusion and the realization of fundamental principles and rights—for current and future generations alike.

On the one hand, this requires environmental and economic policies which are mindful of their impacts on the world of work; on the other hand, social, employment, skills and labour market policies need to incorporate environmental sustainability among their goals so that they contribute to, rather than undermine, the prospects for sustainable enterprises and decent work. Creating institutions and governance mechanisms for environmentally sustainable development at all levels, including ministries of labour and social development, employers' organizations and trade unions, will be essential to achieve the necessary integration and coherence.

Table 4.1 suggests a preliminary framework for identifying the contributions that decent work and the world of work need to make to environmental sustainability from economic, social and environmental perspectives. It begins to identify the guidance on relevant policy measures already contained in international labour standards and major ILO policy statements. While it is clear that much relevant guidance exists, to date it has never been articulated in ways that national and international policy-makers, the private sector or indeed the ILO constituents themselves can act on.

The Rio+20 outcome document, the Cancún Agreements on climate change and a growing number of national policy statements call for decent work and a just transition to low-carbon economies to be recognized as a central goal of, as well as a driver for, sustainable development.

The final chapter of this book summarizes its main findings regarding concepts, research findings and lessons from practical experience with policies and practices for greening businesses and economies around the world in ways that are also conducive to the creation of decent work and to social inclusion.

5
Major findings

The findings of research and the numerous lessons on enterprise development and policy from around the world presented in this book demonstrate that there are both compelling reasons and a solid conceptual foundation for addressing the challenges of decent work for all and of environmental sustainability together. There is also a substantial and growing knowledge base, so that business leaders and policy-makers alike have at their disposal a wealth of effective policy instruments and business strategies.

In order to advance towards sustainable development and socially inclusive low-carbon economies on the scale and at the speed required, the concepts, goals and policy instruments need to be transformed into public policy, business models and enterprise practices. Decisive and ambitious policy action requires a clear and stable policy signal to the private sector. Such a stable framework of policies and incentives can only emerge if there is a strong societal consensus on the goals, the principles to guide the transition and the most effective policy measures to achieve it.

This chapter will show that the indispensable political consensus on ways to achieve the transformation of economies and labour markets has emerged between governments, employers and trade unions around the world. It is reflected in the conclusions unanimously adopted at the 102nd Session of the ILC in 2013. This chapter highlights elements of the conclusions which are particularly relevant to the implementation of the SDGs and of the international climate agreement expected at the end of 2015.[1]

1   The full text of the ILC conclusions is reproduced in Annex II.

5.1 The imperative of environmental sustainability and decent work

5.1.1 Making the economy environmentally sustainable is no longer optional, it is a necessity

Environmental sustainability and decent work for all are two of the defining challenges of the twenty-first century. They need to be addressed urgently and together.

From a social development and in particular a labour market perspective, as well as from a broad sustainable development perspective, a greener economy is no longer an optional goal, but has become an urgent necessity. Escalating resource use, rising pollution, growing scarcity of fresh water and fertile land, accelerating loss of biodiversity, and climate change caused by the current model of development are unsustainable trends and are breaching ever more planetary boundaries.

The social and economic damage caused by environmental degradation has the potential to undo many of the gains in development and poverty reduction achieved over the past decades. This is already evident in the loss of jobs and incomes due to severe weather events. Future climate change impacts are likely to curb economic output and reduce productivity, thereby undermining the viability of businesses and destroying jobs and livelihoods. ILO research puts the economic losses from climate change caused by additional emission under a BAU scenario at 7.2 per cent by 2050. Studies by the OECD and the World Bank which include health effects and other damage to individuals arrive at even higher losses. The sectors most threatened by climate change, such as agriculture, forestry and fisheries, employ well over 1 billion workers, about one-third of world employment, and harbour most of the world's poor.

The environment thus strongly and directly interacts with unresolved social challenges such as massive unemployment, underemployment and working poverty. The widespread lack of basic social protection, and inadequate provision of health and sanitation, add complexity to resolving environmental challenges and increase the vulnerability of many people.

The discussion about greening the economy has long been marred by the assumption that environmental protection may come at the expense of social goals such as the creation and protection of jobs or the reduction of poverty. It has become increasingly clear, however, that environmental and social goals go hand in hand and can reinforce each other. This book provides evidence from a wide range of sectors and countries at all levels of development to underscore this conclusion.

5.1.2 Environmental sustainability is intimately linked with social and labour market outcomes

A decade of research and analysis has led to a much greater understanding of the drivers which link the environment and outcomes for social development and labour markets. It is increasingly possible to analyse and indeed anticipate how environmental factors and policies lead to changes in production and consumption patterns in economies which translate into structural change in economies. These affect the volume as well as the quality of employment and may also impact the levels and distribution of incomes.

Addressing the environmental and social challenges together can create powerful synergies for jobs and incomes. Greater environmental sustainability can drive investment, economic growth and job creation. However, the transition to a greener economy can clearly also imply employment losses, particularly when it involves a wholesale shift in the economic development model of large companies, sectors and countries. Not only the net effects, but also the gains and losses which produce them need to be understood and addressed.

Transitions can also impact the quality of employment. This is critical for sustainable development. The jobs created in the process must be not only green but also decent—that is, they need to provide adequate incomes and social protection, respect the rights of workers and give them a say in decisions which will affect their lives.

Whether the overall effect on the number of jobs is positive or negative will depend on the complex interplay of various factors, including overall demand, investment and trade flows, employment elasticity, and the mix of policies adopted by governments. These dynamics of the quantity and quality of employment linked to environmental impacts and policies can be analysed with a range of analytical tools, in particular macroeconomic models such as input–output and social accounting matrices, as well as dynamic full economy models. Analysis and the monitoring of progress towards environmental sustainability will be greatly facilitated by better data, including for green jobs, based on the operational definition adopted by the International Conference of Labour Statisticians in 2013 (ILO, 2013a).

5.1.3 Environmental sustainability must become a reality in all enterprises across economies, but some sectors are key and green jobs play a pivotal role for achieving it

The emerging understanding and analysis of the environmental challenges and potential solutions makes it clear that no single measure, policy or sector is capable of bringing about environmental sustainability in one country, let alone globally. Because of the linkages between enterprises and economic sectors, greening must be achieved in all enterprises and across economies.

This recognition notwithstanding, eight sectors stand out as heavy consumers of resources, significant polluters and large employers. They are agriculture, forestry, fisheries, energy, resource-intensive manufacturing, recycling, building and transport. Together they employ about 1.5 billion workers, half the global workforce. They also generate at least three-quarters of all GHG emissions in most economies.

While technology plays an important role, environmental sustainability will remain an elusive goal without the active involvement of hundreds of thousands of managers and many millions of workers in enterprises around the world. Workers who directly contribute to reducing the environmental impact of their enterprises or who help to restore ecosystems and their services are key actors in this transformation. These green jobs exist in green sectors, but also as key occupations in all other sectors of the economy. Identifying and tracking these green jobs is critical to ensure that the transition can happen in enterprises and workplaces and also to monitor progress of the economy as a whole.

The drive towards environmental sustainability can be a significant avenue for more and better jobs, social inclusion and poverty reduction. Positive outcomes are eminently possible if opportunities are seized and challenges addressed to bring about a smooth and just transition to sustainable economies.

5.2 The drive towards environmental sustainability creates three major opportunities for labour markets and social inclusion

5.2.1 Considerable net employment gains are possible

The shift to a sustainable, greener economy offers major opportunities for job creation and for social development. A range of studies at global, regional and country levels, reviewed in this book and summarized in Annex I, table A1, support the broad conclusion that considerable net employment gains either have already been realized or can be achieved by making economies more environmentally sustainable compared with a BAU development path. The potential gains identified are in the order of 0.5–2 per cent of the global workforce, or 15–60 million additional jobs.

Gains may be higher in emerging economies and developing countries, which are not as burdened as industrialized countries with the need to make the transition away from heavy fossil fuel use and polluting or resource-intensive infrastructures. Instead, they can leapfrog directly to resource-efficient and environmentally friendly technology and infrastructure, which have become cost-effective over recent decades and are now superior to conventional methods in many areas.

These findings support the double-dividend hypothesis, according to which policy measures can achieve economic benefits (in particular employment gains) and environmental improvements at the same time.

The most pessimistic findings from some studies are that net employment gains or losses would be so insignificant as to be neutral. Even so, employment will likely be more sustainable, with higher job security and fewer social costs and other negative externalities. Moreover, a number of studies suggest that more ambitious and well-coordinated greening strategies could lead to even higher net gains in employment than those found by most researchers.

5.2.2 Better jobs for hundreds of millions of workers in key sectors are both possible and essential

Overall, jobs in the production of green goods and services gained in the transition to a greener economy tend to be of better quality. They typically involve higher levels of qualification, improved safety and health at work, and higher pay than comparable jobs in conventional parts of the economy, as research in China, Germany, Spain and the United States has found.

However, in a number of economic sectors that are key for environmental and for social development there is an urgent need to couple the greening of economic activities with an improvement in working conditions. Agriculture, waste management and recycling, and building construction stand out. All of them are significant employers, but many workers in these sectors toil in poverty and strenuous, and offer little in the way of job security or social benefits. Efforts to upgrade and formalize employment are essential to achieve eco-efficiency and environmental sustainability. They will also greatly advance social inclusion.

In agriculture, the sector on which most of the world's poor depend, environmental challenges can be met by training and supporting some 400 million small-scale farmers to adopt productive farming methods with a low environmental impact. The majority of the 15–20 million waste management and recycling workers in the world are informal waste-pickers in developing countries. Recycling will only become a truly green activity with greater job formalization, which will help improve working conditions, safety and health, and earnings, as Brazil's experience shows. In the construction industry, emerging and developing countries can leapfrog to more energy-efficient new buildings that avoid a legacy of high energy, water and resource consumption. But working conditions and skills levels for many of the over 110 million construction workers globally need to be improved along with greening of construction techniques and materials. Where governments and employers fail to invest in workers, investments in technology, equipment and infrastructure underperform.

5.2.3 Proactive environmental policies can create economic opportunity, help to reduce poverty and advance social inclusion

Renewable energy is now the most cost-effective way to provide clean, modern energy to the 1.3 billion people who do not have it, most in Africa and South Asia. Access to clean energy for all as envisaged under the SDGs can create badly needed employment in the production of that energy, greatly improve productivity and open up entirely new business opportunities in poor areas. Initiatives such as those involving solar home systems in Bangladesh and solar water heaters in Brazil's "My Home, My Life" programme show how this can be done on a large scale.

Likewise, investments in the rehabilitation of stressed natural resources and the restoration of ecosystem services through public works programmes or payments for environmental services can make a direct contribution to poverty reduction, as illustrated by the EPWP in South Africa and the rural employment guarantee under the MGNREGA in India.

5.2.4 The transition to environmentally sustainable economies and societies should be guided by agreed principles

In recent years, a rapidly growing number of countries have embarked on strategies and policies for environmental sustainability, a shift to a green economy or green growth (for an overview, see Annex I, table A2). The conclusions of the 2013 ILC agreed on a set of principles to guide these transformations:

- Strong social consensus on the goal and pathways to sustainability is fundamental. Social dialogue has to be an integral part of the institutional framework for policy-making and implementation at all levels. Adequate, informed and ongoing consultation should take place with all relevant stakeholders.

- Policies must respect, promote and realize fundamental principles and rights at work.

- Policies and programmes need to take into account the strong gender dimension of many environmental challenges and opportunities. Specific gender policies should be considered in order to promote equitable outcomes.

- Coherent policies across the economic, environmental, social, education/training and labour portfolios need to provide an enabling environment for enterprises, workers, investors and consumers to embrace and drive the transition towards environmentally sustainable and inclusive economies and societies.

- These coherent policies also need to provide a just transition framework for all to promote the creation of more decent jobs, including as appropriate: anticipating impacts on employment, adequate and sustainable social protection for job losses and displacement, skills development and social dialogue, including the effective exercise of the right to organize and bargain collectively.

- There is no "one size fits all". Policies and programmes need to be designed in line with the specific conditions of countries, including their stage of development, economic sectors and types and sizes of enterprises.

- In implementing sustainable development strategies, it is important to foster international cooperation among countries.

This book has shown how these principles have been and can be applied in policy-making and implementation, in economic sectors, in enterprises and at workplaces.

5.3 Challenges for labour markets and social inclusion can be identified and must be managed

The industrialized countries in particular may experience some negative job effects associated with environmental reforms. Challenges to creating decent work and increasing social inclusion in the context of sustainable development arise in four broad areas:

1. Impacts of environmental policies on resource-intensive industries

2. Enabling SMEs to navigate the shift to a greener economy

3. Climate change and its threat to jobs and livelihoods

4. Adverse income distribution effects originating from energy poverty

However, several country and sector experiences suggest these can be minimized through the choice of appropriate instruments for environmental policies and complementary labour market and social policies. As noted earlier, improved data, suitable economic modelling and dialogue with the social partners who are close to economic realities can greatly help in identifying and managing these challenges.

5.3.1 Increasing eco-efficiency in resource-intensive industries protects jobs

The sectors experiencing the most direct impacts of environmental policies are resource- and energy-intensive industries, as well as primary industries such as forestry and fisheries, to the extent that they overtax their natural resource base. A small number of industries are responsible for the bulk of pollutants and carbon emissions, yet in most countries they offer relatively limited employment.

Improving the energy and materials productivity of these resource-intensive industries can secure their future viability, improve competitiveness, protect existing jobs and generate new ones. One area with great potential is the use of CHP, which could create around 2 million jobs worldwide.

To succeed in raising resource productivity, it is essential that companies' workforces are empowered to identify ways to cut emissions and waste, as the experience of companies such as 3M in the United States and LG Electronics in the Republic of Korea shows. However, goal-setting through innovative public policy also plays a critical role. Japan's "Top Runner" programme, for example, has pushed the electronics sector into vastly increased efficiency of electronic products through dynamic standards that are set by committees of representatives from manufacturing industry, unions, consumers and universities.

5.3.2 Targeted support for SMEs protects existing jobs and helps to create new ones

SMEs represent over two-thirds of global permanent employment, create almost all new jobs and are an important source of innovation. However, compared with large firms, they often do not have adequate access to information about green markets and skills programmes, or to new technologies and finance. They also face much greater difficulties in compensating for rising energy and raw material costs, and in adjusting to new environmental standards. Better organization, in the form of cooperatives, business associations or partnerships along value chains, can play an important role in helping SMEs to meet the sustainability challenge.

Policies that enable SMEs to successfully navigate the shift to a greener economy have been initiated in a number of countries, including many EU countries, Malaysia, the Philippines, Singapore, Sri Lanka and the United States. Development of technical and also of management skills is an important factor in this context. Especially in developing countries, the owners and employees of small businesses tend to have insufficient business skills.

5.3.3 Lessons learned from earlier shifts need to be used to achieve a just transition to environmental sustainability

It is worth emphasizing that, thus far, greening efforts have been a relatively minor factor in any employment losses. Industries such as mining, fossil-fuel-based energy, iron and steel, and others have seen job losses driven primarily by other factors, including increasing automation, rising labour productivity, and structural shifts in the context of deregulation and globalization processes.

The shifts induced by climate change policies are expected to be much smaller than the 20 per cent job reallocation OECD countries have experienced over the last two decades as a result of globalization, according to a study in the OECD context. While the overall impact may be limited, it is likely to fall disproportionately on industries which have been strongly affected by earlier structural transformation and where the workers and communities which depend on them have few alternative economic opportunities. This can cause hardship and social exclusion and increase the cost of the transformation. It can also generate political resistance to change which is necessary and beneficial for society and the economy as a whole.

Where job losses in the move towards sustainability cannot be prevented, a just transition is a key objective. Central to facilitating a just transition is the early identification of affected regions, industries, enterprises and workers. Governments, business and labour need to work together to identify potential adjustment pressures as early as possible, map likely impacts, inform affected workers proactively, and adopt timely and targeted retraining/skills upgrading efforts, labour market policies and income support measures.

In situations where particular local and regional economies are heavily dependent on shrinking industries, efforts to diversify these economies are needed to allow them to more readily absorb relocating workers. This is particularly important for workers who have limited skills or skills that are difficult to transfer to another industry, and those who are otherwise limited in their geographical mobility.

Experience from past major restructuring efforts in countries around the world points to social security and skill development, as well as diversification and creation of alternative employment opportunities, as keys to a successful outcome. Dialogue, close cooperation and partnerships between the public and private sectors have been hallmarks of successful transitions in, for example, the sugar industry in Brazil (mechanization of cane harvesting), the forest industry in China (logging ban), commercial fishing in

Norway (overfishing), the coalmining industry in Poland (globalization) and the steel industry in the United Kingdom (modernization).

5.3.4 The loss of jobs and livelihoods due to climate change must be averted

While there are understandable worries about the employment impacts of climate policies, the lack of such action is likely to have much more profound impacts on jobs. Climate change will affect enterprises and workers in locations exposed to storms, floods, droughts and fires, including some of the world's largest cities, many of which are located in coastal areas and flood plains. Farmers will have to cope with declining agricultural yields in many areas of the world, especially where rain-fed crop cultivation predominates.

The impacts are already visible in the often massive disruption of economic activity, the loss of infrastructure and productive assets in enterprises, and the forced relocation of enterprises and populations. While large numbers of jobs and livelihoods are at risk, very little specific work has been done to date to map and quantify these effects. Assessments of the likely employment and social impacts of climate change need to be conducted systematically.

Even if the worst consequences of climate change can be avoided through drastic emissions reductions, impacts will be felt for a long time to come. Adaptation therefore becomes increasingly important. However, existing policies and strategies such as the NAPAs still pay little attention to the employment and income dimensions. Better income security and income replacement for vulnerable groups through insurance, such as in the Philippines' Climate Change Adaptation Project, or large-scale public employment programmes, such as the MGNREGA in India, EPWP in South Africa or PSNP in Ethiopia, make critical links between enterprise survival, employment, social protection and the restoration and protection of natural resources, and can thus be useful models.

5.3.5 Socially regressive effects of environmental policies need to be compensated for

Policies required to "get prices right" so they reflect the true cost of energy and resource consumption, such as energy or carbon taxes and the abolition of energy subsidies, affect poor households disproportionately because they spend a much higher share of their income on energy than the average. Similarly, restrictions on the use of natural resources may undermine the livelihoods of poor groups who tend to depend much more on them. Targeted transfers as part of social protection floors and/or increased access to energy-efficient housing and transport, as in Brazil's "Bolsa Família" and "Bolsa Verde" schemes and the social housing programme, not only help to compensate for regressive effects but can also enhance environmental sustainability while promoting social inclusion.

5.3.6 Social and labour market outcomes do not occur by default: policies matter

Modelling and practical experience alike indicate that the labour market impacts of environmental policies are largely a function of the policies applied. Social policies matter as much as environmental policies, and indeed fulfil a critical role in the transition to greener economies. Policy coherence is thus essential. This requires coordination across policy areas such as environment, infrastructure, housing, energy, agriculture and rural development, social protection and employment. It is important that policy-makers take a holistic view that integrates key environmental, social and economic objectives.

Neither the number nor the quality of jobs created is an automatic outcome. Large-scale green job creation requires ambitious environmental targets, which help mobilize growing investment. Eco-taxes put a price on emissions and resource consumption and thus can help internalize external costs in ways that help drive the transition to greener practices. Millions of net new jobs could be created globally if a tax on CO_2 emissions were imposed and the resulting revenues were used to cut labour taxes. This type of environmental tax reform, or "eco-tax", is a powerful tool to achieve economic, environmental and social goals at the same time.

A number of other policy areas play important roles as well. These include creating markets for green goods and services through public works programmes, government procurement and a wide range of sector-specific policy tools. Among these are measures such as feed-in tariffs for renewable energy, building codes, minimum energy efficiency requirements for consumer appliances, zoning of land-use, fishing quotas and many others that fulfil a standard- and norm-setting function.

5.3.7 Competent enterprises and skilled workers are key to green success

Green jobs are not merely the passive outcome of investments in more efficient, less polluting economic activities. Rather, a successful green economy requires competent enterprises with skilled and motivated workers. Well-trained workers are central to the success of greening all aspects of the economy, whether in occupations within agriculture and forestry, manufacturing, technical innovation (R&D), or a wide variety of services including finance, logistics and procurement. What is required is not only initial training and education, which raise environmental awareness, enhance STEM skills and introduce the tools and methods relevant for environmental sustainability, but a lifelong process of honing, imparting and further developing skills.

Moreover, occupational health and environmental impacts beyond the workplace are often intricately linked, such as when major industrial accidents release massive amounts of harmful substances such as chemicals, heavy metals or oil. There are major opportunities to reduce exposure to traditional OSH hazards, to prevent the emergence of new ones and to avoid negative impacts on the wider environment.

Many green jobs are skills-intensive. For example, the construction of energy- and resource-efficient buildings requires competent, skilled workers. Poorly installed equipment and materials mean that expected gains in efficiency fail to materialize, as a study from California shows. Worker training is part of the remedy, but government policies—setting and enforcing standards—are needed to ensure that employers compete on the basis of quality rather than on that of cost alone.

Similar lessons hold in other parts of the green economy, such as the renewable energy industry. The looming skills gap in that sector needs to be addressed to secure a bright future for renewables. Failure to do so could threaten to slow the pace of future expansion, or translate into low-quality installations, which could harm the reliability and thus the public reputation of renewable energy technologies.

Meeting the challenge of developing a green economy is impossible without the active involvement and empowerment of millions of people in the workplace. This requires stepped-up skill-building and training efforts by governments, the education sector and private businesses, from classroom curricula to on-the-job learning. In many instances it will require initiatives to upgrade the competencies of enterprises and of workers, as well as the quality of the jobs, in order to reduce turnover among skilled workers.

5.3.8 Workers and employers need to be organized, consulted and empowered

A wide variety of cases demonstrate how important it is that workers, beyond individually acquiring appropriate skills, are well organized. Traditional trade unions, newer forms such as the Self-Employed Women's Association (SEWA) in India and other forms of organization such as cooperatives can all help generate employment opportunities as well as facilitate efforts to improve working conditions and social inclusion.

Experiences in Brazil, Colombia and Sri Lanka, among others, underscore the point that waste-picker cooperatives and enterprises facilitate formalization. Especially if supported by local or national legislation, this can create significant opportunities for safer working conditions, higher earnings and broader societal acceptance of waste-pickers—who typically contribute net economic benefits to their municipalities.

The organization of farmers is an important prerequisite for giving rural communities a voice in policy-making processes around the greening of agriculture. Organization is also critical for implementing low-environmental-impact farming methods, which require that access to know-how, inputs, finance and markets at fair prices be secured. This is illustrated by the experience of cooperatives such as the Oromia Coffee Growers in Ethiopia and the Kuapa Kokoo cocoa farmers in Ghana, as well as cooperatives growing carbon-neutral coffee in Costa Rica and India.

In the context of biofuels projects in developing countries, smallholders can improve their negotiating position *vis-à-vis* outside investors by organizing farmers' associations, thereby avoiding outcomes that may lead to loss of land and other forms of displacement by large monoculture operations. This is a conclusion supported by the experience of sugarcane outgrower associations in Tanzania. In the community of Mtibwa, the share of outgrowers with annual incomes below the government's minimum wage fell from 63 per cent in 1997–98 to 23 per cent in 2005–06. Run by elected representatives, the association offers training, access to finance, and support in the procurement of inputs and the negotiation of fair prices with company management (Matango, 2006).

Cooperatives and other types of social organization can enhance community access to energy, as examples from a range of countries show. These include Argentina's Sociedad Cooperativa Popular Limitada de Comodoro Rivadavia (SCPL), which owns the country's largest wind park. In Germany, the largest energy cooperative has 22,000 members and more than 100,000 clients. Bangladesh's Rural Electrification Programme (REP) includes approximately 70 energy cooperatives which generate and distribute electricity, and employ about 16,000 people.

Finally, organized workers and employers can inspire and drive greening of entire economic sectors and countries. Experience has been gathered in existing national forums in countries including France, Germany, the Republic of Korea, South Africa, Spain and the United States. For example, Germany's large-scale building energy efficiency renovation programme originated in a "pact for the environment and for jobs" between trade unions and employers in the building sector and NGOs. The programme has mobilized investments of over €120 billion to date, sufficient to continuously support as many as 300,000 jobs in the building industry and its suppliers.

5.3.9 Greening policies need to be designed by and for women

Greening policies need to be gender sensitive—designed to ensure not only that women's needs and interests are included, but also that women have an adequate voice in related decision-making.

For instance, many informal waste-pickers are women. There is evidence that they are working at the lower end of the informal economy and that their income levels are substantially below those of men. Organizing and social inclusion efforts for waste-pickers need to take into account the gender dimension.

Similarly, in efforts towards rural development and greening agriculture, special provision must be made for the inclusion of women farmers, who account for an estimated 43 per cent of the global agricultural labour force. In developing countries, women produce 60–80 per cent of the food but own less than 2 per cent of the land. For true sustainability, these massive imbalances must be rectified (Nierenberg and Burney, 2012).

In rural areas of developing countries, many girls and women spend long hours of back-breaking work collecting firewood, an activity that prevents them from pursuing education and income-generating activities. Women not only bear the heavy physical load of gathering firewood, they are also most exposed to the dangerous air pollutants that result from cooking and lighting homes with traditional biomass and kerosene. Modern forms of renewable energy help reduce these health burdens and improve women's social and economic opportunities.

However, as the example of SHS in Bangladesh illustrates, women are not just passive beneficiaries of renewable energy deployment. More than 1,000 female technicians have been trained to assemble, install and maintain solar systems, and the 50 or so Green Technology Centres are run by female engineers.

5.3.10 The right mix of policies is country-specific

A greener economy requires different practices in most sectors, enterprises and workplaces as well as structural change across the entire economy. A greener economy is in principle compatible with good labour market and social development outcomes, but requires the right set of policies and institutions capable of implementing them. What is appropriate and where priorities lie are judgements strongly influenced by the resource endowments, opportunities and constraints of a national economy and labour market.

There is no one-size-fits-all policy recipe, and the right mix of policies is very much country-specific. Countries and regions with large shares of resource-intensive and high-emitting industries face different challenges from those with a lighter legacy of unsustainable production patterns. Individual countries therefore need customized policy packages in tune with their particular mix of strengths and weaknesses.

Macroeconomic fiscal and monetary policies can be a powerful driver of green investment and net job creation. They provide price signals and incentives through measures such as eco-taxes, price guarantees, subsidies, regulations and public investment. **Sectoral policies** generally rely on environmental regulations, financial incentives and mandates. Industrial policy has been successfully used to support the shift to a greener economy by a number of countries, including Brazil (biofuels), China (all renewables), Denmark (wind), Germany (green buildings among others), Japan (green transport) and Spain (wind and solar).

Social and labour policies for a green transition ideally combine social protection, employment, skills development, and active and passive labour market policies. **Social protection** measures provide a buffer for people who need to undergo adjustments, such as the adoption of sustainable practices, acquisition of new skills, relocation to new jobs, enhancement of resilience, or other adaptations to socially disruptive changes. **Vocational training and skills development** are needed to avoid growing shortages of adequately skilled workers and to enhance individuals' employability in the evolving green economy. Skills upgrading, reskilling and the promotion of "portable skills" are all core needs. **Active labour market programmes** such as jobsearch assistance, job counselling, training and improved labour market information may need to be either simply augmented or specifically tailored to assist in the green transition.

Policies to enable **sustainable enterprise development** are important because the social, economic and environmental dimensions of sustainable development come together inseparably in enterprises and workplaces. As the green economy develops, it is also essential that the **occupational safety and health of workers are integral aspects.**

5.4 There is an urgent need for a fairer, more inclusive and environmentally sustainable development model

As the international community readies itself with the SDGs to adopt and implement the first truly global development agenda, and with the expected outcome of COP21, the first global and ambitious climate agreement, there is an urgent need for a more integrated vision and practice of development.

Given the scale and urgency of these environmental and employment challenges, it is clear that the world will have neither the resources nor the time to tackle them separately or consecutively. Tackling them jointly is not an option, but a necessity. There is thus an urgent need for a fairer, more inclusive and environmentally sustainable development model.

Such a model recognizes that the four pillars of the Decent Work Agenda—social dialogue, social protection, rights at work and productive employment—are indispensable building blocks of sustainable development and must be at the centre of policies for strong, sustainable and inclusive growth and development.

It will also preserve the environment for current and future generations and respect planetary boundaries. In line with this vision, the greening of economies presents many opportunities to achieve social objectives: it has the potential to be a new engine of growth, both in advanced and developing economies, and a net generator of decent green jobs that can contribute significantly to the eradication of poverty and to social inclusion.

The conclusions of the 2013 ILC give specific meaning to the objectives and intent regarding the creation of decent work for all and a just transition contained in both the outcome of the Rio+20 summit and the negotiating text for the climate agreement to be reached at the end of 2015. This global consensus reached by governments, employers' organizations and trade unions of 185 member countries of the ILO provides a firm basis and concrete guidance to governments on principles, effective policies and good practices. They can also inform business, in particular in view of SDG 8, which brings together decent work and economic growth with an emphasis on the role of the private sector.

Governments, employers and workers are not passive bystanders, but rather agents of change. They can develop new ways of working that safeguard the environment for present and future generations, eradicate poverty and promote social justice by fostering sustainable enterprises and creating decent work for all. Sustainable development as envisaged by the Rio+20 summit, including the shift to a low-carbon economy, and the implementation of the SDGs and of a global climate agreement, are only possible with the active engagement of the world of work.

Annex I: Tables

Table A1 Estimated employment effects of greening the economy

Country	Model and employment effects
Australia	• An additional 770,000 jobs by 2030 (a gain of 5–6% by 2030) could be created by an emissions trading system coupled with government incentives, relative to an approach relying on carbon markets only. • 2.5 million jobs could be created by 2025 by reducing GHG emissions 60–100% by 2050, while "Factor 4" resource efficiency offers gains of 3.3 million jobs over the next 20 years, and 7.5 million by 2050. • Construction and transport jobs are projected to grow significantly faster than the national average.
Brazil	• Employment is expected to increase by 1.13% annually between 2010 and 2030, and GDP could increase 0.5% per year on average by reducing pasture areas and protecting forests.
China	• Some 6.8 million direct and indirect jobs could be created by meeting government wind, solar and hydropower targets. • Losses from reduction in energy intensity of industry could be outstripped by almost 10 million jobs through increased employment in renewable industry and through shifting from basic industries towards services.
Croatia	• Investments of €10.6 billion in energy-efficient buildings, biomass, solar thermal systems and wind energy could by 2020 create approximately 14,500 new direct jobs, in addition to 65,000 indirect and induced jobs, according to a 2010 assessment by UNDP. Most of the indirect and induced jobs would be in biomass utilization.

Country	Model and employment effects
European Union	• More than 0.5 million net jobs could be created over 2014–20 by investing 14% of the total EU budget in renewable energy, nature conservation, green buildings and sustainable transport (about 130,000 jobs per €1 billion); shifting investment from current patterns to green sectors could increase job creation per euro by a factor of three. • The EU could add between 1.4 and 2.8 million jobs compared with BAU by reducing the total material requirements of its economy by 17% (every percentage point reduction in resource use could lead to up to 100,000–200,000 new jobs). • A 1.3% increase in employment and 8% decline in CO_2 emissions between 1990 and 2010 generated by increased energy taxes, according to one economic model. A 0.6% rise in employment and 4.4% decline in CO_2 emissions through increased energy prices and lower labour costs, according to another model. • An increase in employment (by up to 0.5%) could be brought about by a carbon tax in six EU countries to reduce energy demand and carbon emissions, while raising GDP (despite some negative short-term transition effects). • The EU's Energy Roadmap to 2050, which aims to achieve 80–95% reductions in GHG emissions, could increase total employment by up to 1.5% (depending on the specific scenario), principally in the construction sector. • Some 400,000 new jobs could be created in the building construction sector by meeting the requirements of the EU Energy Efficiency Directive.
France	• Recent studies estimate that 230,000 workers need to be trained per year through 2020 if objectives are to be reached (130,000 existing professionals + 100,000 new entrants).
Germany	• An increase in employment of 0.55% and a 2% cut in CO_2 emissions between 1999 and 2010, by recycling energy tax revenue to subsidize social security contributions levied on labour. • Slight positive employment effects and a sharp fall in CO_2 emissions in response to an increase in the tax rates and the abolition of eco-tax exemptions. • Some 250,000 jobs were created by ecological tax reform over the period 1999–2003, particularly in labour-intensive sectors, while reducing fuel consumption and CO_2 emissions by 7% and 2–2.5%, respectively.
Indonesia	• A 2% GDP annual green investment in energy, transportation and forestry could generate between 938,984 and 1,270,390 jobs in four sectors with decent working conditions, many being green jobs.
Republic of Korea	• Some 11.8 to 14.7 million new jobs could be created by 2020 through US$97 billion in public investment committed for 2009–13 in support of a green transition.
Lebanon	• Employment gains projected by 2020: in forestry, 15,000; waste management, 2,500; construction, 2,800; energy, 4,000.
Mauritius	• Significantly higher employment can be generated in green activities versus conventional ones per million rupees of final demand: 5% more jobs in agriculture, 67% more in manufacturing and textiles, over 600% more in tourism/hotel services, and 75% more in renewable energy.

Country	Model and employment effects
Mexico	• The Ministry of Energy estimated the potential of clean energy over the period 2012–20. It estimated potential direct, indirect and induced employment gains at about 175,000 jobs—many in construction, the commercial sector, metal products, and scientific and technical professions. Some 48,000 jobs were projected for wind power, 47,200 for co-generation, 36,700 for geothermal, 31,000 for biomass and 12,400 for solar PV.
Norway	• Net employment gains of 0.5–1.5% could be realized through CO_2 mitigation actions that reduce emissions by 20% over the period 2008–20, when revenues from carbon pricing are used to reduce social contributions (with exact results depending on the policy package considered).
Poland	• A programme of energy efficiency modernization, reducing building energy consumption by 64–89%, could create 344,000 net new jobs (taking into account jobs lost in coalmining and elsewhere) by 2020.
South Africa	• Some 98,000 new direct jobs can be created in the short term (2011–12), 255,000 in the medium term (2013–17) and 462,000 in the long term (2018–25) through low-carbon energy generation, energy and resource efficiency, emission and pollution mitigation, and natural resources management. • Over 106,000 new renewable energy jobs can be created by 2030 under an ambitious "energy revolution scenario" (compared with only 7,500 in the IEA's reference (BAU) scenario); total energy employment (including coal export jobs) would be 56% higher than in the IEA reference scenario.
United States	• Some 2.7 million jobs have been created in the "clean economy" industry in recent years, mostly among low- and middle-skilled workers, in the largest US metropolitan areas. • Some 2 million jobs can be created by investing US$100 billion in green recovery measures—four times more than would result by spending the same amount in the oil industry. • A net gain of 1.7 million jobs (2.5 million gained in the clean energy sector, with 800,000 jobs lost in the fossil fuel industries) could result from a US$150 billion green investment programme. • A gain of 918,000 to 1.9 million jobs by 2020 is possible through appropriate climate and clean energy policies, depending on the rigours and effectiveness of the provisions. • More than 4 million FTE job-years can be created by 2030 with aggressive energy efficiency measures combined with a 30% Renewable Portfolio Standard (RPS) target for renewable energy; non-fossil-fuel technologies create more jobs per unit of energy than coal and natural gas. • Investing about US$200 billion annually (US$110 billion in renewable energy; US$90 billion in energy efficiency) to reduce energy-related CO_2 emissions by 40% over 20 years could generate 4.2 million jobs (2.7 million net employment), and lower the unemployment rate by 1.5 percentage points.

Sources: Australia: ACF and ACTU (2009); Hatfield-Dodds et al. (2008). Brazil: de Gouvello (2010). China: GCN (2010). Croatia: UNDP (2010d). European Union: Daly, Pieterse and Medhurst (2011); GWS (2011); ILO and IILS (2009); Andersen and Ekins (2009); Cambridge Econometrics, et al. (2013); EC (2014). France: Establie D'Argencé, Herold and Le Marois (2014), ch. 14. Germany: Bach et al. (2002); Frohn et al. (2003); Bach et al. (2001). Indonesia: ITUC (2012). Republic of Korea: Global Green Growth Institute (2011). Lebanon: ILO (2012i). Mauritius: ILO (2012b). Mexico: SENER (2012). Norway: OECD (2012c). Poland: Institute for Eco-development (n.d.). South Africa: Maia et al. (2011); Rutowitz (2010). United States: Muro et al. (2011); Pollin et al. (2008); Pollin, Heintz and Garett-Peltier (2009); Roland-Holst and Karhl (2009); Wei et al. (2010); Pollin et al. (2014).

Table A2   National initiatives for environmental sustainability, green economy or green growth

Country	Examples of green economy or green growth initiatives
Barbados	• The National Strategic Plan 2006–25 includes "Building a green economy–strengthening the physical infrastructure and preserving the environment" and "Building social capital" as two of six strategic goals. The plan contains strategies to create new businesses and expand existing enterprises on a sustainable basis, supported by a modern synergistic manpower planning framework for decent work and the creation of quality jobs. A scoping study (June 2014) assessed the potential for greening the economy and jobs, examining the enabling conditions for a transition to a green economy.
Brazil	• The national poverty eradication strategy (2011) reflects green opportunities, including social housing, green protection grants (Bolsa Verde) and the formalization of 250,000 recycling workers linked to the National Solid Waste Policy established by law in 2010.
Cambodia	• The national Green Growth Roadmap (2010) aims in the short term (2–5 years) to help stimulate the economy, save and create jobs, protect vulnerable groups and improve environmental sustainability. It recognizes investment in human capital as a key precondition for sustained economic growth, including training for green and decent jobs to enhance the greening of the economy and improve the stock of human capital in Cambodia. In March 2013, the government approved a strategic plan for green growth in the period 2013–30.
China	• The 12th Five-Year Plan (2011–15) set as key themes the rebalancing of the economy, reducing social inequality and protecting the environment. There are plans to invest US$468 billion in greening key economic sectors, in particular waste recycling and reutilization, clean technologies and renewable energy. An estimated 35,000 enterprises and institutions in environment protection and its related industries employ 3 million workers. Employment and skills policies for green jobs are in preparation.
European Union	• Europe 2020 (2010–20), a European strategy for smart, sustainable and inclusive growth, sets key targets covering employment, education, research and innovation, social inclusion and poverty reduction, and climate/energy. Employment targets include the following: 75% of the population aged 20–64 should be employed while meeting the EU's objective of 20% of renewable sources; meeting the 20% target on energy efficiency by 2020 would create over 1 million new jobs. The EC adopted a Green Employment Initiative in July 2014, laying out an integrated framework focused on six priority areas: bridging skills gaps; anticipating and securing transitions; supporting job creation; increasing data quality and monitoring; promoting social dialogue; and strengthening international cooperation.
Ethiopia	• The Climate Resilient Green Economy Initiative (2011–25) seeks to achieve middle-income status by 2025 in a climate-resilient green economy. The initiative promotes socio-economic targets such as rural development; health; the creation of employment in high value-added production; and rural employment. It also supports the local production of efficient stoves, afforestation/reforestation as well as forest management, and the farming of livestock, in particular poultry.

Country	Examples of green economy or green growth initiatives
France	• Under the "Grenelle de l'Environnement" (Environment Round Table) (2009–20), more than US$600 billion is being committed to support green measures and over 300,000 direct jobs have so far been created. In the building sector, the top-down "Plan Bâtiment Grenelle" strategy was combined with local authorities' bottom-up role (Alliance Villes Emploi), with some 33 local action plans focused on training, awareness raising and local development strategies.
Germany	• The objectives of the 2011 energy policy (Energiewende) are: to phase out nuclear energy by 2020 and increase energy efficiency; and to increase renewable energy sources in gross electricity consumption from 17% in 2010 to at least 35% by 2020. About 370,000 workers were employed in renewable energy in 2013 (though the solar sector suffered job losses in solar PV) and another 300,000 in energy-efficient building construction.
India	• The National Action Plan on Climate Change outlines existing and future policies and programmes for climate mitigation and adaptation. The plan identifies eight core "national missions" including solar energy, agriculture, water and habitat, running through to 2017. • The MGNREGA supports several of the missions through a vast public works programme mostly oriented to environmental protection and conservation, benefiting 50 million households in 2012–13, up from 21 million in 2006–07.
Indonesia	• Through its National Action Plan Addressing Climate Change (2007) based on a triple-track strategy which is pro-poor, pro-job and pro-growth, Indonesia has voluntarily committed to reducing its GHG emissions by at least 26%, and up to 41% by 2020, with international support. A Climate Change Sectoral Roadmap including provision for green jobs and skills has been developed to mainstream climate change in the Indonesian national midterm development plan (2010–14), while a National Action Plan on Mitigation and Adaptation to Climate Change on Public Works consists of policies, strategies and programmes to lower impacts of climate change.
Malaysia	• The 10th Malaysia Plan (2011–15) sets out a programme of economic reforms which are expected to facilitate the growth of new industrial sectors, particularly in green technologies. It includes enterprise promotion. An assessment of employment potential is under way.
Mauritius	• The Maurice Ile Durable (MID) (2008–28) long-term vision for sustainable development encapsulates five major themes: energy, education, environment, equity and employment. Government institutions and employers' organizations have included green jobs, skills and enterprises in their strategies.
Mexico	• Mexico established "promoting sustainable development, green growth and the fight against climate change" as one of the priorities of its presidency of the G20 in 2012. A Special Climate Change Programme (2009–12) set a target of cutting national GHG emissions by 50% by 2050 compared to 2000, supported by programmes to replace almost 2 million refrigerators, air-conditioning units and inefficient light bulbs. Mexico's Environmental Leadership for Competitiveness—a programme to improve the competitiveness of value chains and of SMEs through environmental management—benefited 651 businesses up to 2010, generating 923 million pesos (over US$70 million) of savings per year and creating 5,758 permanent jobs. A comprehensive green economy and green jobs assessment, and the identification of indicators to support green growth policies, are under way.

Country	Examples of green economy or green growth initiatives
Morocco	• The Solar Plan (2009–20) aims to reduce Morocco's energy imports by installing 2 GW from solar power by 2020 while supporting economic growth and creating employment; and to achieve industrial integration of concentrated solar power technologies.
Philippines	• The National Climate Change Action Plan (2011–28) includes a specific output on increased productive employment and livelihood opportunities in climate-smart industries and services. Activities programmed aim to develop and improve the matching of labour force skills to climate-smart industry demand; develop a system of monitoring and reporting green job creation and employment; and review and develop innovative financing mechanisms for sustainable livelihoods in rural and climate-change-vulnerable areas.
Republic of Korea	• The plans Road to Our Future: Green Growth, National Strategy and Five Year Plan for Green Growth (2009–13) were expected to generate some 810,000 green jobs by 2013 and foster competitiveness of the Korean economy in technologies that reduce energy dependence, enhance climate resilience and promote a low-carbon growth path.
South Africa	• The Green Economy Accord (2011), adopted as one of the accords under South Africa's New Growth Path, was signed by representatives of the South African Government, business representatives, organized labour and the community constituency at the Parliament of South Africa in November 2011. The accord sets the goal of creating at least 300,000 jobs in the green economy by 2020, including activities that green the economy in manufacturing, energy efficiency, recycling, transport and energy generation. A series of "Working for …" programmes launched by the Department of Environmental Affairs generated 24,000 green jobs by 2012, a number expected to grow to 95,000 in 2017 and 230,000 in 2025.
Sri Lanka	• The National Human Resource and Employment Policy adopted in October 2012 spans critical sectors of the economy, including those that have potential to create green jobs. Technical and financial support will be offered to entrepreneurs, including SMEs, to explore green business opportunities.
United Arab Emirates	• A long-term national initiative, "A Green Economy for Sustainable Development" (2012–21), aims to position the country as a centre for the export and re-export of green products and technologies through programmes and policies in the areas of energy, agriculture, investment, sustainable transport and construction.
United Kingdom	• The Low Carbon Transition Plan: National Strategy for Climate and Energy (2009–20) aims to make a necessary transition to a low-carbon economy through the creation of new business and employment opportunities in renewable energy and building, among other areas, and to achieve a 34% cut in emissions from 1990 levels by 2020.
United States	• The American Recovery and Reinvestment Act (2009) allocated up to US$100 billion to green investments, with a Green Jobs Act that provides for training for workers and entrepreneurs in green sectors such as energy efficiency, renewable energies and sustainable construction.

Annex II: International Labour Conference, 102nd Session, Geneva, 2013

Resolution concerning sustainable development, decent work and green jobs[1]

The General Conference of the International Labour Organization, meeting in Geneva at its 102nd Session, 2013,

Having undertaken a general discussion on the basis of Report V, *Sustainable development, decent work and green jobs*,

1. Adopts the following conclusions; and

2. Invites the Governing Body of the International Labour Office to give due consideration to them in planning future work and to request the Director-General to take them into account when preparing future programme and budget proposals and to give effect to them, to the extent possible, when implementing the Programme and Budget for the 2014–15 biennium.

1 Adopted on 19 June 2013. See http://www.ilo.org/ilc/ILCSessions/102/reports/committee-reports/WCMS_216378/lang--en/index.htm, pp. 66-78.

Conclusions concerning achieving decent work, green jobs and sustainable development

Our vision

1. The four pillars of the Decent Work Agenda—social dialogue, social protection, rights at work and employment—are indispensable building blocks of sustainable development and must be at the centre of policies for strong, sustainable and inclusive growth and development.

2. Sustainable development means that the needs of the present generation should be met without compromising the ability of future generations to meet their own needs. Sustainable development has three dimensions—economic, social and environmental—which are interrelated, of equal importance and must be addressed together.

3. Sharing a common global purpose, there are different approaches, models and tools available to each country, in accordance with its national circumstances and priorities to achieve sustainable development in its three dimensions, which is our overarching goal.

4. A just transition for all towards an environmentally sustainable economy, as described in this document, needs to be well managed and contribute to the goals of decent work for all, social inclusion and the eradication of poverty.

5. Decent work, poverty eradication and environmental sustainability are three of the defining challenges of the twenty-first century. Economies must be productive to meet the needs of the world's growing population. Societies must be inclusive, providing opportunities for decent work for all, reducing inequalities and effectively eliminating poverty.

6. When referring to the greening of economies, enterprises and jobs, we consider it in the context of sustainable development and poverty eradication. This is one of the important tools for achieving sustainable development and could provide options for policy-making. In this context, we welcome the document "The

Future We Want" adopted by the United Nations Conference on Sustainable Development (Rio+20).

7. The greening of economies presents many opportunities to achieve social objectives: it has the potential to be a new engine of growth, both in advanced and developing economies, and a net generator of decent green jobs that can contribute significantly to poverty eradication and social inclusion. The greening of economies will enhance our ability to manage natural resources sustainably, increase energy efficiency and reduce waste, while addressing inequalities and enhancing resilience. The greening of jobs and the promotion of green jobs, both in traditional and emerging sectors, will foster a competitive, low-carbon, environmentally sustainable economy and patterns of sustainable consumption and production, and contribute to the fight against climate change.

8. Managed well, transitions to environmentally and socially sustainable economies can become a strong driver of job creation, job upgrading, social justice and poverty eradication. Greening all enterprises and jobs by introducing more energy and resource efficient practices, avoiding pollution and managing natural resources sustainably leads to innovation, enhances resilience and generates savings which drive new investment and employment.

9. Sustainable development is only possible with the active engagement of the world of work. Governments, employers and workers are not passive bystanders, but rather agents of change, who are able to develop new ways of working that safeguard the environment for present and future generations, eradicate poverty and promote social justice by fostering sustainable enterprises and creating decent work for all.

10. The path to environmentally sustainable development involves a wide range of efforts and activities from the ILO and member States, who have widely varying capabilities and ability to act in accordance with the reality of each State. In that context, cooperation, information sharing and joint action within the mandate of the ILO will be valuable.

11. We recall the principle of common but differentiated responsibilities as set out in the Rio Declaration on Environment and Development (1992).

Opportunities and challenges

12. In the transition to environmentally sustainable economies and societies, the world of work can benefit from some major opportunities, for example:

a. net gains in total employment from realizing the potential to create significant numbers of additional decent jobs through investments into environmentally sustainable production and consumption and management of natural resources;

b. improvements in job quality and incomes on a large scale from more productive processes as well as greener products and services in sectors like agriculture, construction, recycling and tourism;

c. social inclusion through improved access to affordable, environmentally sustainable energy and payments for environmental services, for instance, which are of particular relevance to women and residents in rural areas;

and faces some major challenges, for example:

d. economic restructuring, resulting in the displacement of workers and possible job losses and job creation attributable to the greening of enterprises and workplaces;

e. the need for enterprises, workplaces and communities to adapt to climate change to avoid loss of assets and livelihoods and involuntary migration; and

f. adverse effects on the incomes of poor households from higher energy and commodity prices.

Given the scale and urgency of these environmental and employment challenges, it is clear that the world will have neither the resources nor the time to tackle them separately or consecutively. Tackling them jointly is not an option, but a necessity.

Guiding principles

13. The following principles should guide the transition to environmentally sustainable economies and societies:

a. Strong social consensus on the goal and pathways to sustainability is fundamental. Social dialogue has to be an integral part of the institutional framework for policy-making and implementation at all levels. Adequate, informed and ongoing consultation should take place with all relevant stakeholders.

b. Policies must respect, promote and realize fundamental principles and rights at work.

c. Policies and programmes need to take into account the strong gender dimension of many environmental challenges and opportunities. Specific gender policies should be considered in order to promote equitable outcomes.

d. Coherent policies across the economic, environmental, social, education/training and labour portfolios need to provide an enabling environment for enterprises, workers, investors and consumers to embrace and drive the transition towards environmentally sustainable and inclusive economies and societies.

e. These coherent policies also need to provide a just transition framework for all to promote the creation of more decent jobs, including as appropriate: anticipating impacts on employment, adequate and sustainable social protection for job losses and displacement, skills development and social dialogue, including the effective exercise of the right to organize and bargain collectively.

f. There is no "one-size-fits-all". Policies and programmes need to be designed in line with the specific conditions of countries, including their stage of development, economic sectors and types and sizes of enterprises.

g. In implementing sustainable development strategies, it is important to foster international cooperation among countries. In this context, we recall the outcome document of the United Nations Conference on Sustainable Development (Rio+20), including section VI on means of implementation.

Key policy areas and institutional arrangements for a just transition for all

14. The following elements constitute a basic framework to address the challenges of a just transition for all:

1. The greening of economies in the context of sustainable development and poverty eradication will require a country-specific mix of macroeconomic, industrial, sectoral and labour policies that create an enabling environment for sustainable enterprises to prosper and create decent work opportunities by mobilizing and directing public and private investment towards environmentally sustainable activities. The aim should be to generate decent jobs all along the supply chain, in dynamic, high value added sectors which stimulate the upgrading of jobs and skills as well as job creation and improved productivity in more labour-intensive industries that offer employment opportunities on a wide scale.

2. As the challenge cuts across several domains, there is a need for mainstreaming sustainable development across all areas and for cooperation and coordination between employment authorities and their counterparts in various fields, including finance, planning, environment, energy, transport, health and economic and social development. Institutional arrangements must be adapted to ensure the participation of all relevant stakeholders at the international, national, regional, sectoral and local levels in the building of an appropriate policy framework. Internal coherence should be sought among institutions at the national level, as well as within international institutions at the regional and global levels for the effective integration of the three dimensions of sustainable development.

3. Key policy areas to address environmental, economic and social sustainability simultaneously include:

Macroeconomic and growth policies

a. Macroeconomic and growth policies should promote sustainable production and consumption patterns and place full and productive employment and decent work for all at the centre of economic and social policies. Targeted fiscal policy measures, market-based instruments, public procurement and invest-ment policies can create frameworks for enterprises and inves-tors to adopt or promote more innovative economic practices, based on the sustainable use of resources, leading to more access to economic opportunity and more inclusive labour markets. These policies can have adverse income distribution effects, in particular related to energy poverty, and should be taken into account in the design of policies.

b. Appropriate laws, regulations and other policies aimed at envi-ronmental improvements that lead to resource and energy efficiencies and the prevention of environmental and social degradation can align private incentives with public policy objectives and can be cost effective in the long term. Legisla-tive and regulatory certainty and the rule of law are needed in order to promote environmental and social sustainabil-ity, while stimulating innovation and investments in human, social and environmental capital. These are the prerequisites for long-term competitiveness and economic prosperity, social cohesion, quality employment and better environmental protection.

Industrial and sectoral policies

c. The greening of economies is a global challenge, but many environmental problems are sectoral and the search for solu-tions and the adoption of policies starts there. Numerous coun-tries have used industrial policy to support the shift to greening their economy. As a complement to macroeconomic policies, industrial and sector-related policies and, when appropriate, public–private partnerships as well as public–public partner-ships are effective in helping to improve both the environ-mental and employment performance of existing businesses and stimulating growth in green products and services. Efforts need to focus on key sectors that are most relevant for envi-ronmental sustainability and job creation in the national econ-omy, such as agriculture, water management and sanitation, forestry, fisheries, energy, resource-intensive industries, recy-cling, waste management, buildings and transport. Targeted measures will be needed to formalize substandard, informal jobs in environment-related sectors, such as recycling and waste management, in order to transform these activities into decent jobs.

d. Sectors often have specific governance instruments and institutions. Because of these shared features, employers and workers engage in collective bargaining and other forms of social dialogue at the sectoral level, all of which present opportunities to pursue economic, environmental and social objectives in an effective way.

Enterprise policies

e. Governments should foster the greening of jobs through regulatory and non-regulatory frameworks that support environmental and social sustainability while stimulating innovation and encouraging investments both at home and abroad. Special attention is needed to ensure that such frameworks provide an enabling environment and assist micro, small and medium-sized enterprises (MSMEs), including cooperatives and entrepreneurs, in making the transition.

f. Most jobs are created by MSMEs, yet little information on making operations more resource efficient and environmentally responsible is specifically targeted to MSMEs. Providing such information in a format easily accessible at this level would greatly strengthen employers' capacity to enhance environmental and labour performance. Regulatory systems should have enforcement capacity and be structured to provide advice to business on how compliance can be achieved.

Skills development

g. There must be strong interaction between the world of work and the world of education and training. The greening of the economy must focus on skills development in order to succeed. Solid technical and vocational education and training systems need to involve industry and trade unions. Access to training helps workers develop the skills needed to transition to new types of jobs or to work with new materials, processes and technologies in their existing jobs. Measures to develop skills that support entrepreneurship, resilience, innovation in enterprises, including MSMEs, and their transition to sustainable practices are critical factors of success.

h. Education and training for green jobs presupposes an approach based on comprehensive lifelong learning. National skills development and employment policies linked to broader development plans need to incorporate education for environmental awareness with coherent skills strategies to prepare workers, in particular young people, for the future sustainable world of work. Education and training systems should be designed to meet the needs of youth, women, vulnerable workers and workers in rural areas, enabling them to contribute to and benefit from economic diversification and rural economic empowerment. Equally, training programmes need to target displaced workers, those who lost jobs due to greening, to ensure their swift re-entry into the labour market.

Occupational safety and health

i. Many economic activities for environmental sustainability present health and safety risks related to minerals, chemicals, pesticides and others. Ensuring that all, including green jobs, are decent, safe and healthy jobs is a key aspect of improving job quality. Switching from fossil fuels to renewables, for instance, entails changes in the occupational safety and health situation. Occupational safety and health standards and training must be an essential component of all skills training. Practical prevention measures should be adopted at the enterprise level based on risk assessment and principles of elimination and control of hazards. Policies and programmes under national systems for occupational safety and health should be continuously improved in light of the new challenges to ensure that green jobs are safe. Adequate capacity of the labour inspectorate is essential to ensure compliance.

Social protection

j. Sound, comprehensive and sustainable social protection schemes are an integral part of a strategy for transition towards a sustainable development pattern, built on principles of decent work, social justice and social inclusion. They should provide workers displaced by technological change or those affected by natural disasters with income support as well as access to health care and basic services during the transition, and thereby reduce inequalities.

k. Special targeted assistance to groups, regions and occupations affected by the transition is essential. For example, public and private employment programmes can have large multiplier effects by combining employment generation, income support and conservation of natural assets. Social protection policies should be coordinated with vocational training and active labour market policies as an integral part of the policies necessary to ensure the social dimension of a sustainable economy.

Active labour market policies

1. In many ways the green transition will pose challenges similar to those of earlier transitions caused by technological revolutions, globalization and rapid changes in world markets. Active labour market policies can help enterprises and workers, including unemployed workers, meet these challenges. The anticipation of changing labour market demands, through sound labour market information and data collection systems, as well as social dialogue, is essential to helping governments, employers, workers and education and training systems identify the skills needed currently and in the future and to take appropriate measures to provide timely training. Employment services are important for brokering workforce transition to greener occupations and improving the match between labour demand and supply.

Rights

m. International labour standards offer a robust framework for addressing the challenges to the world of work associated with the greening of the economy and, more broadly, with the transition towards sustainable development and poverty eradication. Several international labour standards, including those covering freedom of association and the right to collective bargaining, prohibition of forced labour, child labour and non-discrimination, social dialogue, tripartite consultation, minimum wage, labour administration and inspection, employment policy, human resource development, occupational safety and health, as well as social security are important in this regard (see Appendix).

Social dialogue and tripartism

n. Mechanisms of social dialogue, including the practice of tripartism and collective bargaining, serve as effective tools for the design of policies at all levels. Social dialogue can form a strong basis by building on the commitment of workers and employers to the joint action with governments needed in the transition process.

Role of governments and employers' and workers' organizations

15. Governments and social partners should individually and jointly work for a greener world by:

a. giving due consideration to advocating for the inclusion of decent work, social justice and the greening of all enterprises and jobs in policies and strategies for sustainable development and the eradication of extreme poverty at national and international levels as part of the post-2015 development agenda; and

b. actively promoting and engaging in social dialogue to forge consensus on pathways towards environmental sustainability which also advance decent work.

16. Governments should:

a. provide the policy and regulatory framework to enable sustainable enterprise development and promote inclusive labour markets, social protection, education and training, private and public investments and innovation that reinforce environmentally sustainable development and decent work, including combating unemployment;

b. foster effective institutional arrangements to ensure coherence across relevant policy portfolios as well as the consultation and participation of all relevant stakeholders for the formulation and implementation of policy at the local, national, regional and international levels; and

c. where possible, design and use efficient and effective monitoring and data collection tools and information systems to monitor and evaluate the impact of the greening of the economy on jobs and, where appropriate, share best practices with the ILO so that those best practices can inform the ILO's work in this area.

17. The social partners should:

a. raise awareness and understanding, as well as provide guidance among their members about developments relevant for the greening of enterprises and the creation of decent green jobs;

b. play an active role in the formulation, implementation and monitoring of national sustainable development policies, articulating the pivotal role of employers and workers in bringing about environmental sustainability with decent work and social inclusion;

c. promote the active participation of their members in social dialogue at enterprise, sectoral and national levels to assess opportunities and resolve challenges posed by transition; and

d. foster a culture of dialogue and workplace cooperation to improve resource efficiency, reduce waste and apply safe and clean technologies and working methods and improve job quality.

Guidance for the Office

18. The ILO, based on its mandate and its core values, is in a unique position to provide leadership in promoting the Decent Work Agenda as a critical vehicle for achieving sustainable development and poverty eradication.

Research, knowledge development, management and dissemination

19. The ILO should:

a. further develop its research capacity to become a centre of excellence to support evidence-based policy-making on sustainable development and decent work;

b. establish knowledge-sharing activities on successful approaches and good practices, for example, learning from the Green Jobs Programme, in integrating economic, social and environmental concerns at the national, local and enterprise levels;

c. carry out research aiming to assist member States and social partners to assess the impact of greening the economy on job creation, job transition and the quality of work, including through the compilation and wide dissemination of reliable statistics;

d. examine the provisions of international labour standards most relevant to achieving a job-rich, equitable, environmentally sustainable economy, and consolidate them for dissemination in a user-friendly form. We note that in paragraph 24 of these Conclusions, we request that the Governing Body consider the convening of a tripartite meeting of experts to give further guidance on issues related to the greening of economies, green jobs and a just transition for all;

e. provide guidance for MSMEs and cooperatives to green their production processes, including through greater energy efficiency and resource use, possibly in the form of a user-friendly toolkit. This work should be carried out in cooperation with national employers' and workers' organizations;

f. ensure that relevant information is widely disseminated in a user-friendly format to constituents; and

g. make sustainable development a cross-cutting issue in the ILO.

Engagement at the global and regional levels

20. The ILO should:

a. continue to work with relevant global and regional institutions to promote consideration of the Decent Work Agenda in macroeconomic policies in order to give practical application to the decent work dimension of the transition to more sustainable patterns of production and consumption and to facilitate tripartite contributions to it;

b. work with relevant global and regional institutions to develop reliable and consistent statistical data on the three dimensions of sustainable development in order to promote evidence-based decision making;

c. work with relevant global and regional institutions to promote decent work and employment considerations in the design of sustainable development technical assistance provided to countries; and

d. actively support constituents in advocating the inclusion of decent work, poverty eradication and a just transition for all to an environmentally sustainable economy in the post-2015 development agenda.

Country-level action

21. The ILO should:

a. integrate sustainable development, poverty eradication and the transition to an inclusive economy in Decent Work Country Programmes (DWCPs), and UN Development Assistance Frameworks (UNDAFs) and promote their consideration in national development plans in line with the needs of constituents concerned;

b. where applicable, develop strategies to help member States to support the transition from informal to formal employment concentrating particularly in sectors that greatly impact the environment, such as agriculture, waste management and recycling, and building and construction;

c. deliver practical technical support for enterprise development and decent job creation in the context of the greening of the economy and adaptation to climate change including in cooperation with other international, regional and national organizations;

d. support member States in the development of comprehensive social protection systems, including social protection floors, in particular to protect those affected by the changes in the world of work;

e. promote and strengthen social dialogue at sectoral and national levels to promote a just transition for all and the creation of decent work;

f. help member States conduct voluntary employment assessments in order to assist them to promote the development of a workforce with skills that are relevant for jobs in emerging green sectors, or in shifting to more sustainable consumption and production processes; and

g. continue to ensure respect for fundamental principles and rights at work in an inclusive, environmentally sustainable economy.

Capacity building

22. The ILO should:

a. build and strengthen the capacity of governments and social partners on the opportunities, challenges and policy responses for an effective and just transition for all. This would include supporting awareness raising and better understanding of the issues involved;

b. build and strengthen the capacity of employers' organizations to offer services to their members, especially MSMEs, so that enterprises and their value chains are able to capture opportunities in growing markets for environmental goods and services; and

c. build and strengthen the capacity of workers' organizations to protect labour rights, participate in collective bargaining, ensure access to training, and enhance job quality in the transition to an environmentally sustainable economy.

The way forward

23. The ILO should prepare a strategic action plan linking decent work, eradication of poverty, sustainable development and green jobs. This should be a key objective which should inform the ILO's mandate for the future at the time of its centenary. The action plan should indicate how this work will be integrated into the programme and budget implementation and the Strategic Policy Framework (2016–21) providing clear follow-up mechanisms, indicating short-term, medium-term and long-term objectives.

24. Conditional on evidence-based analysis, the Governing Body may wish to consider the convening of a tripartite meeting of experts to give further guidance on issues related to the greening of economies, green jobs and a just transition for all.

Appendix

Some international labour standards and resolutions that may be relevant to a just transition framework

Conventions on fundamental principles and rights at work

- Freedom of Association and Protection of the Right to Organise Convention, 1948 (No. 87)

- Right to Organise and Collective Bargaining Convention, 1949 (No. 98)

- Forced Labour Convention, 1930 (No. 29)

- Abolition of Forced Labour Convention, 1957 (No. 105)

- Equal Remuneration Convention, 1951 (No. 100)

- Discrimination (Employment and Occupation) Convention, 1958 (No. 111)

- Minimum Age Convention, 1973 (No. 138)

- Worst Forms of Child Labour Convention, 1999 (No. 182)

Governance Conventions

- Employment Policy Convention, 1964 (No. 122)
- Labour Inspection Convention, 1947 (No. 81)
- Tripartite Consultation (International Labour Standards) Convention, 1976 (No. 144)
- Labour Inspection (Agriculture) Convention, 1969 (No. 129)

Other technical Conventions

- Social Security (Minimum Standards) Convention, 1952 (No. 102)
- Social Policy (Basic Aims and Standards) Convention, 1962 (No. 117)
- Paid Educational Leave Convention, 1974 (No. 140)
- Human Resources Development Convention, 1975 (No. 142)
- Working Environment (Air Pollution, Noise and Vibration) Convention, 1977 (No. 148)
- Labour Administration Convention, 1978 (No. 150)
- Labour Relations (Public Service) Convention, 1978 (No. 151)
- Collective Bargaining Convention, 1981 (No. 154)
- Occupational Safety and Health Convention, 1981 (No. 155)
- Occupational Health Services Convention, 1985 (No. 161)
- Chemicals Convention, 1990 (No. 170)
- Prevention of Major Industrial Accidents Convention, 1993 (No. 174)
- Promotional Framework for Occupational Safety and Health Convention, 2006 (No. 187)

Recommendations

- Human Resources Development Recommendation, 2004 (No. 195)
- Job Creation in Small and Medium-Sized Enterprises Recommendation, 1998 (No. 189)

- Promotion of Cooperatives Recommendation, 2002 (No. 193)

- Social Protection Floors Recommendation, 2012 (No. 202)

Resolutions

- Resolution concerning the promotion of sustainable enterprises—International Labour Conference, 96th Session, June 2007

- Resolution concerning promotion of rural employment for poverty reduction—International Labour Conference, 97th Session, June 2008

Bibliography

3M Company. 2011. *Sustainability report* (Maplewood, MN).

ACF (Australian Conservation Foundation); ACTU (Australian Council of Trade Unions). 2009. *Creating jobs—cutting pollution: The roadmap for a cleaner, stronger economy* (Melbourne).

Ackerman, F.; Stanton, E.A. 2006. *Climate change: The costs of inaction* (Boston, Tufts University, Global Development and Environment Institute).

AfDB (African Development Bank). 2012. *Facilitating green growth in Africa: Perspectives from the African Development Bank*, discussion paper presented at the Rio+20 Conference, Tunis, 14 June.

—; OECD (Organisation for Economic Co-operation and Development); UN (United Nations); World Bank. 2012. *A toolkit of policy options to support inclusive green growth*, submission to the G20 Development Working Group.

Aguilar, L. 2008. *Is there a connection between gender and climate change?* International Union for Conservation of Nature (IUCN), Office of the Senior Gender Adviser, paper for presentation at the 3rd Global Congress of Women in Politics and Governance, Manila, 19–22 Oct.

Alliance of Indian Wastepickers. 2010. *Livelihoods with dignity* (Pune).

Andersen, M.S.; Ekins, P. 2009. *Carbon-energy taxation: Lessons from Europe* (Oxford, Oxford University Press).

Arthur, C. 2010. "Women solar entrepreneurs transform Bangladesh", in *Policy Innovations*, 16 Aug.

AVINA. 2009. *Brazilian president launches the "Cata Ação" program*, online article. Available at: http://www.avina.net/eng/nota/recycling-in-brazil/.

—. 2010. *Brazil sanctions national policy that formalizes the work of 800,000 recyclers*, online article. Available at: http://www.informeavina2010.org/english/reciclaje.shtml.

Ayyagari, M.; Demirguc-Kunt, A.; Maksimovic, V. 2011. *Small vs. young firms across the world: Contribution to employment, job creation, and growth*, World Bank Policy Research Paper No. 5631 (Washington, DC, World Bank).

Bach, S. et al. 2001. *Die ökologische Steuerreform in Deutschland: Eine modellgestützte Analyse ihrer Wirkungen auf Wirtschaft und Umwelt* (Heidelberg, 2001).

—. et al. 2002. "The effects of environmental fiscal reforms in Germany: A simulation study", in *Energy Policy*, Vol. 30, pp. 803-811.

Barua, D. 2010. Email communication with authors, 23 Feb.

—. 2014. "Financial and social benefits of building energy lending program. Bangladesh success story", Zayed Future Energy Prize presentation, Abu Dhabi, 20 Jan. Available at: http://www.slideshare.net/bgef/abu-dhabi-zefp-stand-presentation-jan-2014-2013.

Bimesdoerfer, K.; Kantz, C.; Siegel, J.R. 2011. *Killing two birds with one stone: Driving green jobs through creating a rural renewable energy systems industry*, paper presented at United Nations Research Institute for Social Development, Conference on Green Economy and Sustainable Development, Geneva, Oct.

BIR (Bureau of International Recycling). 2009. *Once upon a time: The story of BIR, 1948–2008* (Brussels).

Blasing, T.J. 2014. *Recent greenhouse gas concentrations*, Carbon Dioxide Information Analysis Centre (CDIAC), DOI: 10.3334/CDIAC/atg.032 (Oakridge, TN). Available at: http://cdiac.ornl.gov/pns/current_ghg.html.

Bloomberg New Energy Finance. 2014. *Global trends in clean energy finance*, 2 Oct. Available at: http://about.bnef.com/presentations/clean-energy-investment-q3-2014-fact-pack/content/uploads/sites/4/2014/10/Clean-energy-investment—Q3-2014-fact-pack.pdf.

Bonner, C. 2008. "Waste pickers without frontiers", in *South African Labour Bulletin*, Vol. 32, No. 4, pp. 7–9.

Borel-Saladin, J.M.; Turok, I.N. 2013. "The impact of the green economy on jobs in South Africa", in *South African Journal of Science*, Sep.–Oct. Available at: http://www.sajs.co.za/sites/default/files/publications/pdf/Borel-Saladin_News%20and%20Views.pdf.

Bridji, S.; Charpe, M.; Kühn, S. 2011. *Economic transition following an emission tax in a RBC model with endogenous growth* (Geneva, IILS).

Buildings Performance Institute Europe. 2011. *Europe's buildings under the microscope* (Brussels).

Café, C.G. 2009. *Brazil: how the "My Home My Life" programme can help the solar water heater sector* (Global Solar Thermal Energy Council). Available at: http://www.solarthermalworld.org/content/brazil-how-my-home-my-life-programme-requires-qualisol-certified-installers [7 Oct. 2010].

—. 2010. *Brazil: "My Home My Life" programme requires Qualisol certified installers* (Global Solar Thermal Energy Council). Available at: http://www.solarthermalworld.org/content/brazil-my-home-my-life-programme-requires-qualisol-certified-installers [7 Oct. 2010].

—. 2011. *Brazil: Low-income multi-family house with individual solar water heaters and gas back-up* (Global Solar Thermal Energy Council). Available at: http://www.solarthermalworld.org/content/brazil-low-income-multi-family-house-individual-solar-water-heaters-and-gas-back [10 Mar. 2015].

Cambridge Econometrics et al. 2013. *Employment effects of selected scenarios from the energy roadmap 2050*. Final report for the European Commission (Cambridge, UK).

Cardoso, F. 2011. *Brazil: New requirements for solar installations on social housing* (Global Solar Thermal Energy Council).

CASS (Chinese Academy of Social Sciences). 2010. *Study on low carbon development and green employment in China* (Beijing, Institute for Urban and Environmental Studies).

CBI (Confederation of British Industry). 2012. *The colour of growth: Maximising the potential of green business* (London), p. 6. Available at: http://www.cbi.org.uk/media/1552876/energy-climatechangerpt_web.pdf [10 March 2015].

CCICED (China Council for International Cooperation on Environment and Development). 2011. *Development mechanism and policy innovation of China's green economy*, CCICED Task Force Report, CCICED Annual General Meeting, 15–17 Nov.

Chateau, J.; Saint-Martin, A.; Manfredi, T. 2011. *Employment impacts of climate change mitigation policies in OECD: A general-equilibrium perspective*, OECD Environment Working Paper No. 32 (Paris, OECD).

Ciroth, A.; Franze, J. 2011. *LCA of an eco-labeled notebook: Consideration of social and environmental impacts along the entire life cycle* (Berlin, Greendelta).

Croitoru, L.; Sarraf, M. (eds). 2010. *The cost of environmental degradation: Case studies from the Middle East and North Africa* (Washington, DC, World Bank).

Daly, E.; Pieterse, M.; Medhurst, J. 2011. *Evaluating the potential for green jobs in the next multi-annual financial framework* (London, GHK).

De Gobbi, M.S. 2011. *Mainstreaming environmental issues in sustainable enterprises: An exploration of issues, experiences and options*, Employment Working Paper No. 75 (Geneva, ILO).

de Gouvello, C. 2010. *Brazil, low-carbon country: Case study* (Washington, DC, World Bank).

Deutsche Bank Climate Change Advisors and Rockefeller Foundation. 2012. *United States building energy efficiency retrofits: Market sizing and financing models* (New York).

Dias, S.M. 2011. *Overview of the legal framework for inclusion of informal recyclers in solid waste management in Brazil*, Urban Policies Briefing Note No. 8 (Cambridge, MA, Women in Informal Employment Globalizing and Organizing).

—; Alves, F.C.G. 2008. *Integration of the informal recycling sector in solid waste management in Brazil* (Bonn, GTZ).

Díaz, S. et al. 2005. "Biodiversity regulation of ecosystem services", in H. Hassan et al. (eds): *Ecosystems and human well-being: Current state and trends* (Washington, DC, Island Press).

Dobbs, R. et al. 2011. *Resource revolution: Meeting the world's energy, materials, food, and water needs* (New York, McKinsey Global Institute).

EASHW (European Agency for Safety and Health at Work). 2011. *Foresight of new and emerging risks to occupational safety and health associated with new technologies in green jobs by 2020: Phase II—Key technologies* (Luxembourg).

EC (European Commission). 2008. *The Economics of Ecosystems and Biodiversity (TEEB): An interim report* (Brussels).

—. 2010. *Europe 2020: A strategy for smart, sustainable and inclusive growth* (Brussels).

—. 2012. *Employment package: Towards a job-rich recovery* (Brussels).

—. 2014. *Green Employment Initiative: Tapping into the job creation potential of the green economy*, COM(2014) 446 final, Brussels, 2 July. Available at: http://ec.europa.eu/social/BlobServlet?docId=11963&langId=en.

—; ILO (International Labour Office). 2011. *Skills and occupational needs in renewable energy* (Geneva, ILO).

ECDVT (European Centre for the Development of Vocational Training). 2010. *Skills for green jobs*, European synthesis report (Thessaloniki).

ECLAC (Economic Commission for Latin America and the Caribbean). 2009. *Economía del cambio climático en Chile: Síntesis* (Santiago).

—. 2010. *Economics of climate change in Latin America and the Caribbean: Summary 2010* (Santiago).

—; ILO (International Labour Office). 2010. "The employment situation in Latin America and the Caribbean", in *ECLAC/ILO Bulletin*, No. 4, Dec.

The Economist. 2012. "Blow-ups happen: Nuclear plants can be kept safe only by constantly worrying about their danger", 10 Mar. Available at: http://www.economist.com/node/21549095 [10 Mar. 2015].

Education and Training Unit (South Africa). n.d. "The Expanded Public Works Programme". Available at: http://www.etu.org.za/toolbox/docs/government/epwp.html [10 Mar. 2015].

EEA (European Environment Agency). 2005. *Sustainable use and management of natural resources*, EEA Report No. 9 (Copenhagen).

—. 2011. *Earnings, jobs and innovation: The role of recycling in a green economy* (Copenhagen).

172 **DECENT WORK, GREEN JOBS AND THE SUSTAINABLE ECONOMY**

ESID (Effective States and Inclusive Development Research Centre). 2013. "Success and failure in MGNREGA implementation in India", Briefing No. 1/2013 (Manchester, UK). Available at: http://www.effective-states.org/wp-content/uploads/briefing_papers/final-pdfs/esid_bp_1_NREGA.pdf.

Establie D'Argencé, M.; Herold, S.; Le Marois, H. 2014. "Lessons from the project 'Employment Centres and Sustainable Development' in France", in OECD/CEDEFOP, *Greener skills and jobs*, OECD Green Growth Studies (Paris), ch. 14. Available at: http://dx.doi.org/10.1787/9789264208704-en.

Fairtrade Foundation, n.d. "Kuapa Kokoo, Ghana". Available at: http://fairtrade.org.uk/en/farmers-and-workers/cocoa/kuapa-kokoo.

FAO (Food and Agriculture Organization). 2008. *Community based adaptation in action: A case study from Bangladesh* (Rome).

—. 2013. *The state of food and agriculture* (Rome).

—; WFP (World Food Programme). 2012. "Joint statement from FAO, International Fund for Agricultural Development and WFP on international food prices", 4 Sep. Available at: http://www.fao.org/news/story/en/item/155472/icode/.

Fay, M. 2012. *Greening growth: A path to sustainable development*, presentation at an ECOSOC meeting, 12 Mar., based on World Bank country environmental analyses. Available at: http://www.un.org/esa/ffd/ecosoc/springmeetings/2012/Presentation_Fay.pdf.

FoE (Friends of the Earth) UK. 2010. *More jobs, less waste* (London).

Frohn, J. et al. 2003. *Wirkungen umweltpolitischer Massnahmen: Abschätzungen mit zwei ökonometrischen Modellen* (Heidelberg, Physica Verlag).

G20. 2012. *G20 leaders' declaration*, Los Cabos, Mexico.

GCN (Global Climate Network). 2010. *Low-carbon jobs in an interconnected world*, Discussion Paper No. 3 (London).

GHK Consulting. 2009. *The impact of climate change on European employment and skills in the short to medium-term* (London).

Gordon, R.J. 2012. *Is US economic growth over? Faltering innovation confronts the six head-winds*, NBER Working Paper No. 18315 (Cambridge, MA).

Gilligan, D.O.; Hoddinott, J.; Taffesse, A.S. 2009. "The impact of Ethiopia's productive safety net programme and its linkages", in *Journal of Development Studies*, Vol. 45, No. 10, pp. 1684-1706.

Global Green Growth Institute. 2011. *Green growth in motion: Sharing Korea's experience* (Seoul).

—. 2014. *Green growth in practice: Lessons from country experiences* (Seoul, Global Green Growth Best Practice Initiative).

Gough, I. et al. 2011. *The distribution of total greenhouse gas emissions by households in the UK, and some implications for social policy* (London, London School of Economics, Centre for Analysis of Social Exclusion).

Government of Bangladesh. 2008. *Cyclone Sidr in Bangladesh: Damage, loss, and needs assessment for disaster recovery and reconstruction* (Dhaka, Economic Relations Division).

Government of Ethiopia. 2011. *Ethiopia's climate-resilient Green Economy Strategy* (Addis Ababa). Available at: http://www.uncsd2012.org/content/documents/287CRGE%20Ethiopia%20Green%20Economy_Brochure.pdf.

—. 2013. "The Ethiopian Climate Resilience Green Economy (CRGE) strategy", presentation at OECD Expert Workshop on "Climate resilience and economic growth in developing countries", Paris, 24 Apr. Available at: http://www.oecd.org/env/cc/3_OECD%20Ethiopian%20CRGES%20PPt%20Final.pdf.

Government of Germany, n.d. *CO₂—Gebäudesanierung—Energieeffizient Bauen und Sanieren*. Available at: http://www.bundesregierung.de/Webs/Breg/DE/Themen/Energiewende/Energiesparen/CO2-Gebaeudesanierung/_node.html.

Govindan, M.; Bhanot, J. 2012. *Green jobs in India: Potentials and perspectives*, Economy of Tomorrow Series (Bonn: Friedrich Ebert Stiftung).

Greenpeace Energy eG. 2014. "An overview", Mar. Available at: http://www.greenpeace-energy.de/fileadmin/docs/sonstiges/Greenpeace_Energy_Fact_Sheet.pdf.

GRID (Global Resource Information Database)-Arendal. 2002. *Vital climate graphics Africa* (Arendal, Norway).

GWS (Gesellschaft für Wirtschaftliche Strukturforschung). 2011. *Macroeconomic modelling of sustainable development and the links between the economy and the environment* (Osnabrück).

Haque, N. 2014. "Results-based financing: Models, experience and lessons learned. IDCOL solar home system program—Bangladesh", presentation at 6th Africa Carbon Forum, 2 July.

Harsdorff, M.; Lieuw-Kie-Song, M.; Tsukamoto, M. 2011. *Towards an ILO approach to climate change adaptation*, ILO Employment Working Paper No. 104 (Geneva, ILO).

Hatfield-Dodds, S. et al. 2008. *Growing the green collar economy: Skills and labour challenges in reducing our greenhouse gas emissions and national environment footprint* (Canberra, CSIRO Sustainable Ecosystems).

Hersoug, B. 2006. *Always too many? The human side of fishery capacity adjustment in Norway*, presentation at OECD Expert Meeting on the Human Side of Fisheries Adjustment, 19 Oct.

ICC (International Chamber of Commerce). 2012. *Green economy roadmap* (Paris). Available at: http://www.iccwbo.org/Data/Policies/2012/ICC-Green-Economy-Roadmap-best-practices-and-calls-for-collaboration/.

IDCOL (Infrastructure Development Company). n.d. "IDCOL SHS installation under RE program." Available at: http://www.idcol.org/old/bd-map/bangladesh_map/.

IEA (International Energy Agency). 2008. *Combined heat and power: Evaluating the benefits of greater global investment* (Paris, 2008).

—. 2009. *World Energy Outlook 2009* (Paris).

—; UNDP (United Nations Development Programme); UNIDO (United Nations Industrial Development Organization). 2010. *Energy poverty: How to make modern energy access universal?* (Paris, IEA).

ILS (Institute for Labor Studies); MOHRSS (Chinese Ministry of Human Resources and Social Security). 2010. *Study on green employment in China* (Beijing, ILO Office for China and Mongolia).

ILSR (Institute for Local Self-Reliance). 2002. *Recycling means business* (Washington, DC). Available at: http://ilsr.org/recycling-means-business/.

infoDev. 2010. *India Climate Innovation Center: CIC. A business plan for the financing and implementation of a CIC in India*. Available at: https://infodev.org/infodev-files/resource/InfodevDocuments_1009.pdf.

—. n.d. *Climate Technology Program eUpdate*. Available at: http://www.infodev.org/infodev-files/infodev_ctp_eupdate.pdf.

Institute for Eco-development. n.d. "Nowe miejsca pracy dzięki efektywności energetycznej" ("New jobs through energy efficiency"). Available at: http://www.ine-isd.org.pl/theme/UploadFiles/File/projekty/EE_PRACAl.pdf.

Intelligent Energy Europe. 2012. "BUILD UP Skills—Belgium—analysis of the national status quo", Aug. Available at: http://buildupskills.eu/sites/default/files/BUSBelgiumNSQ.pdf.

ILO (International Labour Office). 2007a. *Decent work for sustainable development*, Report of the Director-General, Report 1 (A), International Labour Conference, 96th Session, Geneva, 2007 (Geneva).

—. 2007b. *Conclusions concerning the promotion of sustainable enterprises*, International Labour Conference, 96th Session, Geneva, 2007 (Geneva).

—. 2008. *Cyclone Sidr: Preliminary assessment of the impact on decent employment and proposed recovery strategy, focusing on non-farm livelihoods* (Geneva).

—. 2009a. *Recovering from the crisis: A Global Jobs Pact*, International Labour Conference, 98th Session, Geneva, 2009 (Geneva).

—. 2009b. *Gender equality at the heart of decent work*, Report VI, International Labour Conference, 98th Session, Geneva, 2009 (Geneva).

—. 2009c. *Green jobs: Improving the climate for gender equality tool* (Geneva).

—. 2010a. "*Gundo lashu* (our victory): Labour-intensive public roads programmes in South Africa", in *World of Work*, No. 70 (Geneva).

—. 2010b. *The impact of climate change on employment: Management of transitions through social dialogue. Case study of social dialogue roundtables on the effects of compliance with the Kyoto Protocol on competitiveness, employment and social cohesion in Spain* (Geneva).

—. 2010c. *Climate change and labour: The need for a "just transition"* (Geneva).

—. 2011a. *Social protection floor for a fair and inclusive globalization*, Report of the Social Protection Floor Advisory Group (Bachelet report) (Geneva).

—. 2011b. *World Social Security Report 2010/11: Providing coverage in times of crisis and beyond* (Geneva).

—. 2011c. *Skills and occupational needs in green building* (Geneva).

—. 2011d. *Promoting decent work in a green economy* (Geneva).

—. 2011e. *Skills for green jobs: A global view* (Geneva).

—. 2011f. *Assessing green jobs potential in developing countries: A practitioner's guide* (Geneva).

—. 2011g. *Greening the global economy: The skills challenge, Skills for Employment policy brief* (Geneva).

—. 2012a. *Global Employment Trends 2012: Preventing a deeper job crisis* (Geneva).

—. 2012b. *Assessing current and potential green jobs: The case of Mauritius, policy brief* (Geneva).

—. 2012c. *Employment creation model in Sri Lanka: Promoting green jobs and livelihoods in municipal solid waste management* (Jakarta).

—. 2012d. *Towards sustainable construction and green jobs in the Gaza Strip* (Geneva).

—. 2012e. *Discussion about the effect given to the decision adopted in November 2011 on the item entitled Green jobs, decent work and sustainable development, with a focus on the implication for the ILO's programme of work of the outcome of the UNCSD 2012 (Rio+20)*, GB.316/POL/3, para. 20, as amended by the Governing Body, Nov.

—. 2012f. *Social dialogue on environmental policy around the globe: A selection of national and regional participatory experiences* (Geneva).

—. 2012g. *Social dialogue: Promoting sound governance, inclusive growth and sustainable development, information note* (Geneva).

—. 2012h. *Built environment and labour: Formulating projects and studies concerning labour issues in greening the sectors of the built environment* (Geneva).

—. 2012i. *Green jobs assessment in Lebanon* (Geneva).

—. 2013a. *Report III, Report of the Conference, 19th International Conference of Labour Statisticians*, Geneva, 2–11 Oct. (Geneva, 2013). Available at: http://ilo.org/global/statistics-and-databases/meetings-and-events/international-conference-of-labour-statisticians/19/WCMS_234124/lang--en/index.htm.

—. 2013b. *Guidelines concerning a statistical definition of employment in the environmental sector adopted by the 19th International Conference of Labour Statisticians* (Geneva, 2013). Available at: http://ilo.org/global/statistics-and-databases/standards-and-guidelines/guidelines-adopted-by-international-conferences-of-labour-statisticians/WCMS_230736/lang--en/index.htm.

—. 2013c. *Recurrent discussion on the strategic objective of social dialogue*, Report VI, International Labour Conference, 102nd Session, Geneva, 2013 (Geneva).

—. 2014. *Global Employment Trends 2014* (Geneva).

—; IILS (International Institute for Labour Studies). 2009. *World of Work Report 2009: The global jobs crisis and beyond* (Geneva, ILO).

—; IILS (International Institute for Labour Studies). 2011. *Towards a greener economy: The social dimensions* (Geneva, ILO).

—; IILS (International Institute for Labour Studies). 2012a. *Working towards sustainable development: Opportunities for decent work and social inclusion in a green economy* (Geneva, ILO).

—; IILS (International Institute for Labour Studies). 2012b. *World of Work Report 2012: Better jobs for a better economy* (Geneva, ILO).

—; OECD (Organisation for Economic Co-operation and Development). 2012. *Sustainable development, green growth and quality employment: Realizing the potential for mutually reinforcing policies*, background paper for the meeting of G20 labour and employment ministers, Guadalajara, Mexico, 17–18 May.

—; World Bank. 2012. *Joint synthesis report: Inventory of policy responses to the financial and economic crisis* (Geneva and Washington, DC).

IMF (International Monetary Fund). 2011. *Who's going green and why? Trends and determinants of green investment*, working paper (Washington, DC).

—. 2014. *World Economic Outlook*, Oct. (Washington, DC).

IPCC (Intergovernmental Panel on Climate Change). 2007. *Fourth assessment report: Climate change (AR4)* (Geneva, UNEP).

—. 2014. *Climate change 2014: Mitigation of climate change. Contribution of Working Group III to the fifth assessment report of the Intergovernmental Panel on Climate Change*, ed. O. Edenhofer et al. (Cambridge, UK, and New York, Cambridge University Press).

IRENA (International Renewable Energy Agency). 2012. *Renewable energy: Jobs and access* (Abu Dhabi).

—. 2013. *Renewable energy and jobs* (Abu Dhabi).

IRLE (Institute for Research on Labor and Employment). 2011. *California workforce education and training needs assessment for energy efficiency, distributed generation, and demand response* (Berkeley, CA).

ITC (International Trade Centre); ILO (International Labour Office). 2010. *Desarrollo sustentable y trabajo decente: Manual formativo para trabajadores de Las Americas* (Turin).

ITUC (International Trade Union Confederation). 2010. *Resolution on combating climate change through sustainable development and just transition* (Brussels). Available at: http://www.ituc-csi.org/resolution-on-combating-climate.html.

—. 2012. *Growing green and decent jobs* (Brussels).

—; DGB (Deutscher Gewerkschaftsbund (German Confederation of Trade Unions); Friedrich Ebert Stiftung. 2014. Trade union workshop on "Achieving decent work in the renewable energy sector", Berlin, 13–14 Oct.

Jaeger, C.C. et al. 2009. *Wege aus der Wachstumskrise* (Potsdam, European Climate Forum).

—. et al. 2011. *A new growth path for Europe: Generating prosperity and jobs in the low-carbon economy*, final report (Potsdam, European Climate Forum).

Jamasb, T.; Meier, H. 2010. *Energy spending and vulnerable households*, EPRG Working Paper 1101, Cambridge Working Paper in Economics 1109 (Cambridge, UK, University of Cambridge Faculty of Economics).

Khullar, M. 2009. "Surviving on scrap", in *Scrap* magazine, Sep.–Oct.

Kim, H.; Han, J.; Park, J. 2012. *Green growth and green jobs in Korea: Potentials and perspectives*, "Economy of Tomorrow" series (Bonn, Friedrich Ebert Stiftung).

Leidreiter, A. 2014. "The feed-in tariff is better than is commonly understood", *Energy Transition* blog, 31 July. Available at: http://energytransition.de/2014/07/the-fit-is-better-than-is-understood/.

Le Quéré, C. et al. 2014. *Global carbon budget 2014*, Earth System Science Data discussions, doi:10.5194/essdd-7-521-2014.

LG Electronics. 2011. *Sustainability report 2010* (Seoul).

Lieuw-Kie-Song, M.R. 2009. *Green jobs for the poor: A public employment approach*, Poverty Reduction Discussion Paper PG/2009/02 (New York, UNDP).

Loudiyi, H. 2010. "Brazil announces phase two of the Growth Acceleration Program", *Growth and crisis blog* (Washington, DC, World Bank). Available at: http://blogs.worldbank.org/growth/node/8715.

Mahapatra, R.; Suchitra, M.; Moyna. 2011. "A million opportunities lost", in *Down to Earth*, 15 Dec.

Maia, J. et al. 2011. *Green jobs: An estimate of the direct employment potential of a greening South African economy* (Sandown, Industrial Development Corporation and Development Bank of South Africa).

Matango, R. 2006. *Mtibwa outgrowers scheme: A model for smallholder cane production in Tanzania*, paper presented to expert meeting, "Enabling small commodity producers in developing countries to reach global markets", UNCTAD Commodities Branch, Geneva, 11–13 Dec. Available at: http://unctad.org/sections/wcmu/docs/c1EM32p16.pdf.

Mattera, P. et al. 2009. *High road or low road? Job quality in the new green economy* (Washington, DC, Good Jobs First).

Mazur, E. 2012. *Green transformation of small businesses: Achieving and going beyond environmental requirements*, OECD Environmental Working Paper No. 47 (Paris, OECD).

Modern Ghana. 2012. "How Fairtrade benefits cocoa farmers: the Kuapa Kokoo experience", 23 Nov. Available at: http://www.modernghana.com/news/432146/1/how-fairtrade-benefits-cocoa-farmers-the-kuapa-kok.html.

MOHRSS (Ministry of Human Resources and Social Security, China). 2010. *China Labour Statistical Yearbook 2010* (Beijing).

—. 2011. *Natural Forest Protection Programme, background information* (Beijing).

MTE/RAIS (Ministério do Trabalho Emprego, Relação Anual de Informações Sociais). n.d. "Annual list of social information" online database.

Muchagata, M. 2014. "Taking inclusiveness as the starting point for green growth: Brazil's Bolsa Verde programme", presentation at OECD forum on "Green growth and sustainable development", Paris, 13 Nov. Available at http://www.oecd.org/greengrowth/ggsd-2014.htm.

Munson, D. 2009. Private communication with Paul Gardiner, 2 Feb. (London, Combined Heat and Power Association).

Muro, M. et al. 2011. *Sizing the clean economy: A national and regional green jobs assessment* (Washington, DC, Brookings Institution).

Namuwoza, C.; Tushemerirwe, H. 2011. "Uganda: Country report 2011", in H. Willer and L. Kilcher (eds): *The world of organic agriculture: Statistics and emerging trends 2011* (Bonn, International Federation of Organic Agriculture Movements).

NDRC (National Development and Reform Commission). 2012. *10,000 enterprises energy saving and low carbon action*, NDRC policy (Beijing) (in Chinese).

Neves, M.F.; Trombin, V.G.; Consoli, M.A. 2010. "Measurement of sugar cane chain in Brazil", in *International Food and Agribusiness Management Review*, Vol. 13, No. 3, pp. 37–54.

Nicola, S. 2014. "China surpasses EU in per-capita pollution for first time", in *Bloomberg News*, 22 Sep.

Nierenberg, D.; Burney, S.A. 2012. "Investing in women farmers", in *Vital Signs Online*, 31 July.

Nordhaus, W. 2007. *The challenge of global warming: Economic models and environmental policy* (New Haven, Conn.: Yale University Press).

NRCIDMC (Norwegian Refugee Council and Internal Displacement Monitoring Centre). 2014. *Global estimates 2014: People displaced by disasters*, Sep. (Geneva).

Nzimakwe, T.I. 2008. "Addressing unemployment and poverty through public works programmes in South Africa", in *International NGO Journal*, Vol. 3(12), pp. 207–212.

OECD (Organisation for Economic Co-operation and Development). 2008. *Gender and sustainable development: Maximizing the economic, social and environmental role of women* (Paris).

—. 2010. *Interim report of the Green Growth Strategy: Implementing our commitment for a sustainable future*, meeting of the OECD Council at ministerial level, 27–28 May (Paris, 2010).

—. 2011. *Towards green growth* (Paris).

—. 2012a. *OECD environmental outlook to 2050: The consequences of inaction* (Paris).

—. 2012b. *Linking renewable energy to rural development* (Paris).

—. 2012c. *Supplemental material for Chapter 4 of the 2012 OECD Employment Outlook: Summary of country responses to the OECD questionnaire on green jobs* (Paris).

—; FAO (Food and Agriculture Organization). 2011. *OECD–FAO Agriculture Outlook 2011–2030* (Paris).

Ortiz Malavasi, R.; Sage Mora, L.F.; Borge Carvajal, C. 2003. *Impacto del programa de pago por servicios ambientales en Costa Rica como medio de reducción de pobreza en los medios rurales* (San José, Costa Rica, Unidad Regional de Asistencia Tecnica).

Parry, M. et al. 2009. *Assessing the costs of adaptation to climate change: A review of the UNFCCC and other recent estimates* (London, International Institute for Environment and Development and Grantham Institute for Climate Change).

Pollin, R.; Heintz, J.; Garett-Peltier, H. 2009. *The economic benefits of investing in clean energy* (Washington, DC, Center for American Progress).

— et al. 2008. *Green recovery: A program to create good jobs and start building in a low-carbon economy* (Amherst, MA, Political Economy Research Institute, University of Massachusetts).

— et al. 2014. *Green growth: A US program for controlling climate change and expanding job opportunities*, Sep. (Washington, DC, Center for American Progress and Political Economy Research Institute).

Preston, G. 2014. "South Africa's Working for … Programmes", presentation at OECD Forum on Green Growth and Sustainable Development, Paris, 13 Nov. Available at: http://www.oecd.org/greengrowth/ggsd-2014.htm.

Qingyi, W. 2010. *Coal industry in China: Evoluement and prospects* (San Francisco, Nautilus Institute, 2000).

Quirion, P.; Demailly, C. 2008. *–30% de CO_2 = +684 000 emplois: l'équation gagnante pour la France* (Paris, WWF France).

Rahmsdorf, S. 2010. "A new view on sea level rise: Has the IPCC underestimated the risk of sea level rise?", in *Nature reports climate change*, 6 Apr. 2010. Available at: http://www.nature.com/climate/2010/1004/full/climate.2010.29.html.

Recycled Energy Development. 2010. *Businesses and advocates unite to promote legislation to strengthen US manufacturing competitiveness*, press release, 12 Apr. (Westmount, Ill.). Available at: http://www.recycled-energy.com/newsroom/press-releases/businesses_promote_legislation_strengthening_manufacturing_competitiveness/.

Reid, H. et al. 2007. *The economic impact of climate change in Namibia: How climate change will affect the contribution of Namibia's natural resources to its economy*, Environmental Economics Programme Discussion Paper 07-02 (London, International Institute for Environment and Development).

Renner, M. 2013. *Renewable electricity jobs: Trends, policies, and key companies*, unpublished report for International Trade Union Confederation (ITUC), Oct.

Republic of Korea. 2012. *Job creation outcomes through implementation of 5-year Green Growth National Plan*, inter-ministerial report (Seoul).

Rockström, J. et al. 2009. "A safe operating space for humanity", in *Nature*, Vol. 461 (24 September 2009), pp. 472-475.

Roland-Holst, D.; Kahrl, F. 2009. *Clean energy and climate policy for US growth and job creation* (Berkeley, University of California).

Rosenfeld, J. et al. 2009. *Averting the next energy crisis: The demand challenge* (NewYork, McKinsey Global Institute).

Rutowitz, J. 2010. *South African energy sector jobs to 2030* (Sydney, Institute for Sustainable Futures, University of Technology).

Sabates-Wheeler, R.; Devereux, S. 2010. "Cash transfers and high food prices: Explaining outcomes on Ethiopia's Productive Safety Net Programme", in *Food Policy*, Vol. 35, No. 4, pp. 274-285.

SANBI (South African National Biodiversity Institute). n.d. "Working for Wetlands programme overview", http://www.sanbi.org/sites/default/files/jobs/documents/Summary%20of%20Rehabplan%20Waterberg.pdf.

Sanghi, S.; Sharma, J. 2014. "Local development strategy, green jobs and skills in the Indian context", in OECD and CEDEFOP, *Greener skills and jobs*, OECD Green Growth Studies (Paris), ch. 12. Available at http://dx.doi.org/10.1787/9789264208704-en.

Schneider, W. 2011. "Alliance for work and environment in Germany", presentation at European Social Partner Conference on "Initiatives involving social partners in Europe on climate change policies and employment", Brussels, 1-2 Mar.

SEBRAE (Serviço Brasileiro de Apoio às Micro e Pequenas Empresas). 2012. *Produção e consumo sustentáveis: Oportunidade e diferencial competitivo a partir do empreendedorismo sustentável* (Brasilia) (in Portuguese).

SENER (Secretaría de Energía, Government of Mexico). 2012. *Iniciativa para el desarrollo de las energías renovables en México* (Mexico City). Available at: http://www.sener.gob.mx/webSener/portal/Default.aspx?id=2333.

Sengenberger, Werner. 2011. *Beyond the measurement of unemployment and underemployment: The case for extending and amending labour market statistics* (Geneva, ILO).

Source Watch. 2011. *Coal and jobs in the United States*, 15 June. Available at: http://www.sourcewatch.org/index.php?title=Coal_and_jobs_in_the_United_States.

South African Department of Environmental Affairs. 2014. "The Department of Environmental Affairs leads the National Green Jobs Dialogue", 10 April. Available at: https://www.environment.gov.za/mediarelease/dea_leads_nationalgreenjobsdialogue.

—. n.d. *About Working for Water*. Available at: http://www.environment.gov.za/projectsprogrammes/wfw.

South African Department of Public Works. 2014. "Expanded Public Works Programme (EPWP) Phase 3", presentation at Green Jobs Summit, 9 April. Available at: https://www.environment.gov.za/sites/default/files/docs/greenjobsdialogue_epwp_phase3.pdf.

Soybean and Corn Advisor. 2011. *Mechanized sugarcane harvest results in rural unemployment*, 10 May. Available at: http://www.soybeansandcorn.com/news/May10_11-Mechanized-Sugarcane-Harvest-Results-in-Rural-Unemployment.

State Council of China. 2002. *Afforestation regulation*, Document No. 367 (Beijing) (in Chinese).

Stern, N. 2007. *The economics of climate change: The Stern review* (Cambridge, UK, Cambridge University Press).

Strietska-Ilina, O. et al. 2011. *Skills for green jobs: A global view*, synthesis report based on 21 country studies (Geneva, ILO).

Summer, S.A.; Layde, P.M. 2009. "Expansion of renewable energy industries and implications for occupational health", in *Journal of the American Medical Association*, Vol. 302, No. 7, 19 Aug., pp. 787–789.

Sustain Labour Foundation. 2008. *Developing renewables—Renewing development: Towards clean, safe and fair energy* (Madrid, 2008).

Suwala, W. 2010. *Lessons learned from the restructuring of Poland's coalmining industry* (Geneva, International Institute for Sustainable Development).

SVTC (Silicon Valley Toxics Coalition). 2009. *Toward a just and sustainable solar energy industry* (San Jose, CA).

—. 2014: *2014 solar scorecard* (San Jose, CA).

Syndex; S. Partner; WMP. 2009. *Climate disturbances, new industrial policies and ways out of the crisis* (Brussels, European Trade Union Confederation).

Tata Steel Europe, 2014. *UK Steel Enterprise: helping our steel communities take the next step.* Available at: http://www.tatasteeleurope.com/en/sustainability/communities/helping-UK-steel-regions.

Tellus Institute. 2011. *More jobs, less pollution: Growing the recycling economy in the US* (Boston).

Ten Brink, P. et al. 2012. *Nature and its role in the transition to a green economy*, TEEB series (London, Institute for European Environmental Policy).

Tovar, P.I. 2014. "Fossil-fuel subsidy reform in Mexico", presentation at OECD Forum on Green Growth and Sustainable Development, Paris, 13 Nov. Available at: http://www.oecd.org/greengrowth/ggsd-2014.htm.

Trabish, H.K. 2011. *The multibillion-dollar value of energy service companies*, 31 Oct. Available at: http://www.greentechmedia.com/articles/read/The-Multi-Billion-Dollar-Value-of-Energy-Service-Companies/.

Tumushabe, G. et al. 2007. *Integrated assessment of Uganda's organic agriculture subsector: Economic opportunities and policy options to mitigate negative socio-economic and environmental impacts* (Kampala, Advocates Coalition for Development and Environment).

UN (United Nations). 1993. *Agenda 21* (New York).

—. 2012. *Sustainable energy for all: A framework for action.* Report of the Secretary-General's High-level Group on Sustainable Energy for All (New York).

UNCSD (United Nations Conference on Sustainable Development). 2012. *The future we want* (New York).

UNCTAD (United Nations Conference on Trade and Development). 2009. *Trade and Environment Review 2009/2010* (New York and Geneva).

—; UNEP (United Nations Environment Programme). 2008. *Organic agriculture and food security in Africa* (New York and Geneva).

UN-DESA (United Nations Department of Economic and Social Affairs). 2009. *Rethinking poverty: Report on the world social situation 2010* (New York, 2009). Available at: http://www.un.org/esa/socdev/rwss/docs/2010/fullreport.pdf.

UNDP (United Nations Development Programme). 2007. *Human Development Report 2007/2008: Fighting climate change: Human solidarity in a divided world* (New York).

—. 2010a. *Gender, climate change and community-based adaptation* (New York).

—. 2010b. *Human Development Report 2010: The real wealth of nations* (New York).

—. 2010c. *Rights-based legal guarantee as development policy: The Mahatma Gandhi National Rural Employment Guarantee Act*, UNDP India discussion paper (New Delhi).

—. 2010d. *Croatia. Green jobs in Croatia: where and how many? Available at: http://www.hr.undp.org/content/dam/croatia/docs/Research%20and%20publications/environment/UNDP-HR-GREEN-JOBS-CROATIA-2014.pdf.

UNEP (United Nations Environment Programme). 2009. *Global green new deal: An update for the G20 Pittsburgh Summit* (Nairobi).

—. 2010a. *Assessing the environmental impacts of consumption and production: Priority products and materials*, International Resource Panel (Paris).

—. 2010b. *Green economy: Developing countries success stories* (Nairobi).

—. 2011a. *Decoupling natural resource use and environmental impacts from economic growth*, International Resource Panel (Paris).

—. 2011b. *Keeping track of our changing environment: From Rio to Rio+20 (1992–2012)* (Nairobi).

—. 2011c. *Towards a green economy: Pathways to sustainable development and poverty eradication* (Nairobi, 2011).

—; GRID (Global Resource Information Database)-Arendal. 2008. *Vital water graphics*, 2nd edn. (Arendal).

—; ILO (International Labour Office); IOE (International Organisation of Employers); ITUC (International Trade Union Confederation). 2008. *Green jobs: Towards decent work in a sustainable, low-carbon world* (Nairobi, UNEP).

—; SETC (Society of Environmental Toxicology and Chemistry). 2009. *Guidelines for social life cycle assessment of products* (Brussels).

UNFCCC (United Nations Framework Convention on Climate Change). 2007. *Climate change: Impacts, vulnerabilities and adaptation in developing countries* (Bonn).

—. 2010. *Report of the conference of the parties on its sixteenth session*, Cancún, 29 Nov.–10 Dec., FCCC/CP/2010/7 (Bonn).

—. 2011. *The Cancún agreements*: Decision 1/CP.16 (15 Mar. 2011), para. I:10. Available at: http://unfccc.int/resource/docs/2010/cop16/eng/07a01.pdf.

—. 2014. *NAPAs received by the secretariat*. Available at: http://unfccc.int/adaptation/workstreams/national_adaptation_programmes_of_action/items/4585.php.

UNICA (União da Indústria de Cana-de-Açúcar). 2009. "UNICA Launches the Largest Retraining Program Ever Implemented by the Sugar-Energy Sector Anywhere in the World". Press release, 1 June. Available at: http://www.unica.com.br/media-center/2663121192031749047/unica-launches-the-largest-retraining-program-ever-implemented-by-the-sugar-energy-sector-anywhere-in-the-world/.

UNIDO (United Nations Industrial Development Organization). 2009. *Manila Declaration on Green Industry in Asia* (Vienna).

—. 2011a. *UNIDO Green Industry Initiative for sustainable industrial development: An overview of UNIDO's Green Industry Initiative* (Vienna).

—. 2011b. *Green industry for a low-carbon future: Resource use and resource efficiency in emerging economies – A pilot study on trends over the past 25 years* (Vienna).

—. 2011c. *UNIDO green industry: Policies for supporting green industry*, May (Vienna).

UN-REDD (United Nations Collaborative Initiative on Reducing Emissions from Deforestation and Forest Degradation). n.d. *UN-REDD programme regions and partner countries*. Available at: http://www.un-redd.org/partner_countries/tabid/102663/default.aspx.

Ürge-Vorsatz, D. et al. 2010. *Employment impacts of a large-scale deep building energy retrofit programme in Hungary* (Budapest, Central European University).

USBLS (United States Bureau of Labor Statistics). 2012. *Employment in green goods and services—2010*, news release, 22 Mar.

—. n.d. Database: *Employment, hours, and earnings from the current employment statistics survey* (national). Available at: http://www.bls.gov/ces/.

Warner, K. et al. 2008. *Human security, climate change, and environmentally induced migration* (United Nations University, Institute for Environment and Human Security). Available at: http://www.ehs.unu.edu/file/get/4033.

— et al. 2012. *Where the rain falls: Climate change, food and livelihood security, and migration* (United Nations University, Institute for Environment and Human Security). Available at: http://unu.edu/publications/policy-briefs/where-the-rain-falls-climate-change-food-and-livelihood-security-and-migration.html.

Water Resources Group. 2009. *Charting our water future: Economic frameworks to inform decision-making* (New York, McKinsey).

WEF (World Economic Forum). 2012. *Financing green growth in a resource-constrained world: Partnerships for triggering private finance at scale* (Geneva).

Wei, M. et al. 2010. "Putting renewables and energy efficiency to work: How many jobs can the clean energy industry generate in the US?", in *Energy Policy*, Vol. 38, pp. 919-931.

WFP (World Food Programme). 2012. *Productive Safety Net Programme (PSNP)*, fact-sheet, Sep.

WHO (World Health Organization). 2011. *Health in the green economy* (Geneva).

—. 2014: "7 million premature deaths annually linked to air pollution", press release, 25 Mar. (Geneva).

Wilson, D.J. 2012. "Fiscal spending jobs multipliers: Evidence from the 2009 American Recovery and Reinvestment Act", in *American Economic Journal: Economic Policy*, Vol. 4, No. 3, pp. 251-282.

Wissenschaftsladen Bonn. 2010. *Mehr Studiengänge und Jobs denn je—Einstieg in Erneuerbare Energien gelingt leichter*, 29 Oct. Available at: http://www.wila-bildungszentrum.de/de/wilabonn/ueber-uns/presse/pressemitteilungen-archiv/190-mehr-studiengaenge-und-jobs-denn-je-einstieg-in-erneuerbare-energien-gelingt-leichter.html.

World Bank. 2008. *World Development Report 2008: Agriculture for development* (Washington, DC).

—. 2010. *The cost to developing countries of adapting to climate change: New methods and estimates*, Global Report of the Economics of Adaptation to Climate Change Study, consultation draft (Washington, DC).

—. 2012a. *Inclusive green growth: The pathway to sustainable development* (Washington, DC).

—. 2012b. *What a waste: A global review of solid waste management* (Washington, DC, 2012).

—. 2012c. *Moving beyond GDP: How to factor natural capital into economic decision-making*, report of Wealth Accounting and the Valuation of Ecosystem Services (WAVES) (Washington, DC). Available at: http://www.wavespartnership.org/sites/waves/files/images/Moving_Beyond_GDP.pdf.

—. 2012d. *Global Monitoring Report 2012: Food prices, nutrition, and the Millennium Development Goals* (Washington, DC).

—. 2012e. *World Development Report 2013: Jobs* (Washington, DC).

—. 2012f. *Turn down the heat: Why a 4 degree centigrade warmer world must be avoided* (Washington, DC).

—. 2013. *New climate innovation center in Ethiopia transforms challenges into business opportunities*, press release, 2 Dec. Available at: http://www.worldbank.org/en/news/press-release/2013/12/02/new-climate-innovation-center-in-ethiopia-transforms-challenges-into-business-opportunities.

—. 2014a. *Bangladesh receives $78.4 million to install an additional 480,000 solar home systems*, press release, 30 June.

—. 2014b. *Ghana climate innovation center business plan: Building competitive clean technology industries in Ghana*. Available at: http://www.infodev.org/infodev-files/gcic_business_plan_final_27_january_2014.pdf.

—. n.d. *World Bank Group energy portfolio by sector, FY2007–FY2011* (Washington, DC). Available at: http://go.worldbank.org/ERF9QNT660.

World Coal Institute. 2005. *The coal resource: A comprehensive overview of coal* (London).

World Resources Institute. 2012. "Development Banks Commit $175 Billion for Sustainable Transport" (Washington, DC). Available at: http://www.wri.org/our-work/top-outcome/development-banks-commit-175-billion-sustainable-transport.

Yang, Y. 2001. "Impacts and effectiveness of logging bans in natural forests: People's Republic of China", in P.B. Durst et al. (eds): *Forests out of bounds: Impacts and effectiveness of logging bans in natural forests in Asia–Pacific* (Rome, FAO).